CHILDREN'S MATHEMATICS

CHILDREN'S MATHEMATICS

COGNITIVELY GUIDED INSTRUCTION

THOMAS P. CARPENTER
University of Wisconsin-Madison

ELIZABETH FENNEMA
University of Wisconsin-Madison

MEGAN LOEF FRANKE
University of California-Los Angeles

LINDA LEVI
University of Wisconsin-Madison

SUSAN B. EMPSON
University of Texas-Austin

HEINEMANN • PORTSMOUTH, NH

Heinemann
A division of Reed Elsevier Inc.
361 Hanover Street
Portsmouth, NH 03801–3912
http://www.heinemann.com

The National Council of Teachers of Mathematics, Inc.
1906 Association Drive
Reston, VA 20191

Offices and agents throughout the world

The development of the CGI Professional Development Program was supported in part by the National Science Foundation under Grant Numbers MDR-8955346 and MDR-8550236. The opinions expressed are those of the authors and do not necessarily reflect the views of the National Science Foundation.

A set of seven video tapes illustrating the ideas presented in this book can be ordered from the Wisconsin Center for Education Research. The tapes supplement the CDs included with this book. The seven video tapes include 93 examples of individual children solving problems, and 10 classroom episodes with accompanying teacher commentary. One tape provides an overview of CGI including comments from the authors and from teachers who have participated in the program. To order the tapes, contact:

Center Document Service, Room 242
Wisconsin Center for Education Research
1025 W. Johnson St.
Madison, WI 53706
Phone: (608) 265-9698

Library of Congress Cataloging-in-Publication Data

Children's mathematics : cognitively guided instruction / Thomas P.
    Carpenter . . . [et al.].
        p.   cm.
    Includes bibliographical references.
    ISBN 0-325-00137-5
    1. Mathematics—Study and teaching (Primary)   I. Carpenter,
    Thomas P.
    QA135.5.C4947   1999
    372.7'044—dc21   98-49595
                                                                    CIP

Editor: Leigh Peake
Production: Melissa L. Inglis
Cover design: Darci Mehall
Manufacturing: Louise Richardson

Printed in the United States of America on acid-free paper

    05 06 RRD   11 12 13 14 15

CONTENTS

When a child's strategy or classroom example in the text is also viewable on the accompanying CDs, an icon in the margin will refer you to CD 1, Children's Strategies, *or CD 2,* Classroom Episodes.

To Deborah Carey

FOREWORD

One of the first times that I had a conversation with Eliz (Fennema) and Tom (Carpenter) about Cognitively Guided Instruction (CGI), I remember saying that they should tell teachers how students should symbolically represent addition and subtraction. During this conversation, I realized how serious they were about respecting teachers' judgments on particular issues. Since they had little research evidence about representing these situations, they would see how teachers and children handled it. As they worked with teachers, sharing their research knowledge about students' learning of addition and subtraction, they would continue to learn from teachers and children.

Carpenter and Fennema have remained faithful to this position over the fifteen years since that initial conversation and have expanded the mathematical domains in which they have worked. In the foreword to the book *Making Sense* (Hiebert et al. 1997), which highlighted CGI and other research efforts, I described the book as presenting "a position that respects and supports each teacher's knowledge, expertise, and beliefs. It is filled with the expectation that professionals, each with his or her own contributions, will work together as partners" (xv). CGI exemplified this characterization.

As you use this book, you will step into the world of research as a professional who is capable of making decisions about student learning of mathematics. If you are not familiar with this body of research, you will learn how young children develop mathematically. In recognizing how students develop mathematically, you may find yourself asking questions similar to the following: Can students solve problems before we teach them exactly how? Do children move through different ways to solve problems? What affects their choice of strategies? What happens when we teach children a procedure before they have tried to solve problems related to that procedure? What happens when children learn routines that do not make sense to them?

You will begin to rethink who can learn mathematics and what it means to learn mathematics. Are only a few children, perhaps those that easily abstract ideas, able to be successful in mathematics? Are there strands of mathematics in which some children seem to have more success?

You will begin to rethink how you teach mathematics. Do you show children how to do each and every step? Do you encourage children to talk mathematics? Does their talking help build mathematical ideas and skills? Do you allow children to struggle? Do you have children explain their ways of thinking? Do you discuss the differences among different strategies used to solve a problem? Which worked well for this problem? Would it work if the numbers were larger? Which is a more sophisticated strategy? You will also experience times when you question how you teach mathematics. This is healthy, for we should reflect on what we are doing and continue to grow in our knowledge of mathematics, of learning mathematics, and of ways to help children learn mathematics.

This book is about helping you help students make sense of mathematics. My prediction is that you, too, will make more sense of mathematics and more sense of how to teach. If the book is meaningful to you, you will probably have more questions than answers. If you are fortunate enough to teach with colleagues in this way, together you and your colleagues will begin to answer some of these questions. As your students are making sense of mathematical ideas, you will be making sense of your teaching and continuing to grow as you learn from your students, your colleagues, and your reflections.

As I reflect back on that first conversation and even my limited involvement with CGI through the years, I realize the impact it has had on my thinking and teaching. Gone is the time when I thought I had the answers; now I have lots of questions. I am looking forward to using this book with those that I teach and together we will wrestle with our questions. It is my hope that you will do the same. If every student could begin their mathematical schooling by making sense of mathematics, each would have the foundation for a strong and worthwhile mathematics education.

MARY M. LINDQUIST

Past President, National Council of Teachers of Mathematics
Fuller E. Callaway Professor of Mathematics Education,
Columbus State University, Columbus, Georgia

ACKNOWLEDGMENTS

A very special thanks to Penelope Peterson. Without her, Cognitively Guided Instruction would never have existed.

Our thanks for many faithful, intelligent, and hard-working staff members at the Wisconsin Center for Education Research at the University of Wisconsin–Madison, who made significant contributions to CGI: Rebecca Ambrose, Ellen Ansell, Jae-Meen Baek, Jeanie Behrend, Laura Brinker, Deborah A. Carey, P. L. Chiang, Donald Chambers, Rosemary Griffith, Janice Gratch, Judith Hankes, Eric Gutstein, Richard Lehrer, Victoria Jacobs, Cheryl Lubinski, Gregory Thoyre, and Janet Warfield.

Our thanks and appreciation are also extended to those who offered help in the development of this guide: Fae Dremock, Chris Kruger, Margie Pligge, Sydney Raynal, Kay Schultz, and Nancy Vacc.

Many teachers and their students have contributed to the development of CGI. We cannot possibly list all of their names, but the following provided direct help or have been directly quoted or shown in this book:

Ann Badeau	Jennifer Beard	Lynn Behrendt
Sue Berthouex	Mary Bostrom	Kerri Burkey
Cathy Chenoweth	Karen Falkner	Joan Fleming
Brenda Fujikawa	Michelle Garden	Susan Gehn
Almeta Hawkins	Mazie Jenkins	Margaret Jenson
Annie Keith	Virginia Koberstein	Therese Kolan
Barbara Martin	Craig Meyer	Candy Nerge
Mary Paquette	Patricia Rentschler	Kathy Statz
Ruth Steiner	Ken Swift	Francine Tate
Pam Thomas	Carrie Valentine	Dyanne Van Den Heuvel
Barbara Wiesner	Mary Jo Yttri	

INTRODUCTION

It is only when you build from within that you really understand something. If children don't build from within and you just try to explain it to a child then it's not really learned. It is only rote, and that's not really understanding.

Ann Badeau, second-grade teacher

In the past I thought children didn't understand subtraction with regrouping, when what they didn't understand was how to use the process that I was insisting that they use, rather than really understanding the concept of subtraction that might encompass regrouping.

Kerri Burkey, second-grade teacher

Young children are naturally curious and have a desire to make sense of their world. In their early experiences they encounter a variety of situations involving quantities, and at a very early age they begin to recognize relationships involving those quantities. By the time they begin school, most children have started to learn to count and demonstrate remarkable insight about how to use their emerging counting skills to solve problems.

We see children's early mathematical thinking in their solutions to problems that they encounter in their daily lives and in their ability to solve problems that are posed to them. For example, Molly, a four-year-old, shares twelve candies with three friends by distributing them one by one to each of the friends. Jonathan, a beginning kindergartner, solves the following problem by modeling it using chips to represent the candies: "There are seven candies in this jar. How many candies will be left if you eat three of them?" Jonathan counts out seven chips, removes three of them, and counts the chips that are left to find the answer. Although neither Molly nor Jonathan have been taught about division or subtraction, they show a basic understanding of the situations that underlie them, and this understanding can serve as a foundation for them to learn about addition, subtraction, multiplication, and division.

Until recently, we have not clearly recognized how much young children understand about basic number ideas, and instruction in early mathematics too often has not capitalized on their rich store of informal knowledge. As a consequence, the mathematics we have tried to teach in school often has been disconnected from the ways that children think about and solve problems in their daily lives. As Kerri Burkey points out in her quote, children may actually understand the concepts we are trying to teach but be unable to make sense of the specific procedures we are asking them to use. Children do not always think about mathematics in the same ways that adults do. If we want to give children the opportunity to build their understanding from within, we need to understand how children think about mathematics. This book is about understanding how children's mathematical thinking develops and reflecting on how to help children build up their concepts from within. It provides a framework for assessing children's thinking in whole number arithmetic and describes how this thinking evolves over time.

Over the last twenty years we have learned a great deal about how children come to understand basic number concepts. Based on our own research and the work of others, we have been able to map out in some detail how basic number concepts and skills develop in the early grades. For the last dozen years, we have been working with primary grade teachers to help them understand how children's mathematical ideas develop. We have observed how much children are capable of learning when their teachers truly understand children's thinking and provide them an opportunity to build on their own thinking. We also have learned from teachers how important it is for them to have explicit knowledge of children's mathematical thinking. One of the first teachers we worked with commented, "I have always known that it was important to listen to kids, but I never knew what questions to ask or what to listen for."

CHILDREN'S MATHEMATICS

1 | CHILDREN'S MATHEMATICAL THINKING

Initially, young children have quite different conceptions of addition, subtraction, multiplication, and division than adults do. This does not mean that their conceptions are wrong or misguided. In fact their conceptions make a great deal of sense, and they provide a basis for learning basic mathematical concepts and skills with understanding.

This chapter provides a picture of the overarching principles underlying children's thinking. This perspective provides a unifying structure for understanding the more detailed analyses of children's thinking in addition, subtraction, multiplication, and division with single and multidigit numbers in the following chapters.

MODELING THE ACTION
AND RELATIONS IN PROBLEMS

Consider the following problems:

> *Eliz had 8 cookies. She ate 3 of them. How many cookies does Eliz have left?*

> *Eliz has 3 dollars to buy cookies. How many more dollars does she need to earn to have 8 dollars?*

> *Eliz has 3 dollars. Tom has 8 dollars. How many more dollars does Tom have than Eliz?*

Most adults would solve all three of these problems by subtracting three from eight. To young children, however, these are three different problems, which they solve using different strategies. For example, Tanya, a beginning first-grader, solved the first problem with physical objects by putting out eight and removing three of them. She found the answer by counting the ones that remained. For the second problem, she started with a set of three counters and added more until there was a total of eight counters. She counted the five objects that she had added to the initial set to find the answer. For the third problem she made two sets, one containing three counters and one containing eight. She lined them up so that the set of three matched three counters in the set of eight, and counted the unmatched objects in the set of eight. Tanya's strategies for solving these problems are typical of the way that many children her age solve them.

The different solutions to these three problems illustrate that, in the eyes of children, not all addition or subtraction problems are alike. There are important distinctions between different types of addition problems and between different types of subtraction problems, which are reflected in the way that children think about and solve them. However, although Tanya used a different strategy for each problem, there is a common thread that ties the strategies together. In each case, she *directly modeled* the action or relationship described in the problem. The first problem involved the action of removing three from eight, and that is how Tanya modeled the problem. In the second problem, the action was additive, and Tanya started with a set representing the initial quantity and added counters to it. The third problem involved a comparison of two quantities, so Tanya used a strategy for comparing two sets.

Now look at how Tanya solved the following division problems:

Ramon had 12 gumdrops. He put 3 gumdrops on each cupcake. How many cupcakes was he able to put gumdrops on?

There are 20 children in the first-grade class. The teacher wants to divide the class into 4 teams with the same number of children on each team. How many children will be on each team?

For the first problem, Tanya put out twelve counters. Then she put three of them in one group, three more in another, three more in a third group, and the final three made the fourth group. To find the answer, she counted the *groups*. For the second problem, she first put out twenty counters. Then she dealt the counters one by one into four piles. To find the answer, she counted the number of *counters* in one of the piles.

Again, Tanya directly modeled the action described in the problems. In the first case, she made groups of a specified size and counted the groups to find the answer. In the second, she made a given number of groups with the same number in each group and counted the objects in one of the groups to find the answer. The differences in the strategies used to solve the two problems reflect the different actions described in the problems. Although adults may recognize both as division problems, young children initially think of them in terms of the actions or relationships portrayed in the problems.

USING COUNTING STRATEGIES
AND DERIVED NUMBER FACTS

The action and relationships in a problem tend to influence the strategies that children use for an extended period of time, but older children do not always represent all the quantities in a problem with physical objects. Over time, direct modeling strategies give way to more efficient counting strategies, which are generally more abstract ways of modeling a problem. For example, José, another first-grader, solved the same problem that Tanya physically modeled by counting on from three to eight:

> Eliz has 3 dollars to buy cookies. How many more dollars does she need
> to earn to have 8 dollars?

José started counting at three and counted, "3 [pause], 4, 5, 6, 7, 8." As he counted from four to eight, he extended a finger with each count. When he reached eight, he counted the five extended fingers. What distinguishes this solution from Tanya's is that José realized that he did not have to make the initial set of three objects. He could represent the extra dollars needed by the numbers in the counting sequence from four to eight. The trick was to figure out how many numbers there were in that sequence, which he did by keeping track on his fingers. This is a more abstract solution than Tanya used, but the counting sequence still parallels the action in the problem. He solved the problem in which Eliz ate three cookies by counting back from eight, "8 [pause], 7, 6, 5. She has 5 left."

No one taught these counting strategies to José. He invented them himself. The invention of increasingly efficient procedures for representing addition, subtraction, multiplication, and division problems is another kind of problem solving for which young children demonstrate remarkable facility and creativity. Children also demonstrate this skill in the ways they use their developing knowledge of number facts. For example, Zena, another first-grade student, could not recall the number fact 6 + 8 in solving a problem, but she knew that 7 + 7 is 14, so she said, "I take 1 from the 8 and give it to the 6. That makes 7 and 7, and that's 14."

DOING WHAT COMES NATURALLY

All of the strategies we have described come naturally to young children. Children do not have to be taught that a particular strategy goes with a particular type of problem. With opportunity and encouragement, children construct for themselves strategies that model the action or relationships in a problem. Similarly, they do not have to be shown how to count on or be explicitly taught specific derived facts. In an environment that encourages children to use procedures that are meaningful to them, they will construct these strategies for themselves. Virtually all children use the basic strategies described above at various times in the development of their understanding of basic number concepts.

LOOKING AHEAD

The thesis of CGI is that children enter school with a great deal of informal or intuitive knowledge of mathematics that can serve as the basis for developing understanding of the mathematics of the primary school curriculum. Without formal or direct instruction on specific number facts, algorithms, or procedures, children can construct viable solutions to a variety of problems. Basic operations of addition, subtraction, multiplication, and division can be defined in terms of these intuitive problem-solving processes, and symbolic procedures can be developed as extensions of them.

The above examples illustrate how the structure of a problem influences the strategies that children use to solve it. In order to understand how children think about addition, subtraction, multiplication, and division, it is necessary to consider differences among problems. In the chapters that follow, we set forth classification schemes for describing important differences among addition and subtraction problems and multiplication and division problems. These analyses provide a framework for understanding the strategies that children use to solve problems. The discussion starts with an analysis of addition and subtraction problems. Using this analysis, we detail the evolution of children's strategies for solving these problems.

Initially, children model the action and relations in problems, reflecting the distinctions portrayed in the analysis of problem types. Over time, these physical modeling strategies give way to more efficient counting strategies, which are generally more abstract ways of modeling a problem. Eventually children come to rely on number facts, but the learning of number facts is not necessarily a rote skill. It can build upon an understanding of number relations, which are supported by a foundation of number sense developed through using modeling and counting strategies. Chapter 4 portrays a similar picture of the development of multiplication and division concepts. In Chapter 5, we return to the notion of problem solving as modeling and examine it in a broader context. Chapter 6 addresses the development of base-ten number concepts and multidigit algorithms. We end with two chapters that discuss how Cognitively Guided Instruction can be applied in the classroom and an Appendix that describes the research basis for this approach.

2 | ADDITION AND SUBTRACTION
Problem Types

There are important distinctions among different types of addition/subtraction problems that are reflected in the ways that children think about and solve them. The goal of this chapter is to describe a classification scheme for addition and subtraction problems that provides a structure for selecting problems for instruction and interpreting how children solve them.

Although there are a number of ways that word problems can be distinguished from each other, one of the most useful ways of classifying them focuses on the types of action or relationships described in the problems. This classification corresponds to the way that children think about problems. As a result, this scheme distinguishes among problems that children solve differently and provides a way to identify the relative difficulty of various problems.

For addition/subtraction problems, four basic classes of problems can be identified: *Join*, *Separate*, *Part-Part-Whole*, and *Compare*. The number size can vary, as can the theme or context of the problems; however, the basic structure involving actions and relationships remains the same. Join and Separate problems involve action. In Join problems, elements are added to a given set. In Separate problems, elements are removed from a given set. Part-Part-Whole and Compare problems do not involve actions. Part-Part-Whole problems involve the relationship between a set and its two subsets. Compare problems involve comparisons between two disjoint sets. Problems within a class all involve the same type of action upon quantities or relationships between quantities. Within each class, several distinct types of problems can be identified depending upon which quantity is the unknown.

JOIN PROBLEMS

Join problems involve a direct or implied action in which a set is increased by a particular amount. The following is an example of the type of Join problem that teachers commonly use to introduce addition:

3 birds were sitting in a tree. 2 more birds flew onto the tree. How many birds were in the tree then?

The action in the problem takes place over time: There is a starting quantity at Time 1 (the three birds sitting in the tree); a second (or change) quantity is joined to the initial quantity at Time 2 (the two birds that flew onto the tree); the result is a final quantity at Time 3 (the five birds then in the tree).

Although the resulting set of birds is composed of the birds initially in the tree and the birds that joined them, the two sets of birds take on quite different roles in the problem because of the temporal nature of the action. These distinctions are important because children may not initially realize that two birds joining three birds gives the same result as three birds joining two birds. Furthermore, three distinct types of Join problems can be generated by varying which quantity is the unknown (Figure 2.1). Each of these problems represents a different problem to young children. Children use different strategies to solve them, and they vary significantly in difficulty.

FIGURE 2.1
Join Problem Types

Unknown	Example
Result Unknown	Robin had 5 toy cars. Her parents gave her 2 more toy cars for her birthday. How many toy cars did she have then?
Change Unknown	Robin had 5 toy cars. Her parents gave her some more toy cars for her birthday. Then she had 7 toy cars. How many toy cars did Robin's parents give her for her birthday?
Start Unknown	Robin had some toy cars. Her parents gave her 2 more toy cars for her birthday. Then she had 7 toy cars. How many toy cars did Robin have before her birthday?

SEPARATE PROBLEMS

Separate problems are similar to Join problems in many respects. There is an action that takes place over time, but in this case the initial quantity is decreased rather than increased. As with Join problems, there are three distinct quantities in Separate problems, any one of which can be the unknown. There is a starting quantity, a change quantity (the amount removed), and the result. Figure 2.2 on the following page gives examples of the three distinct types of Separate problems that can be generated by varying the unknown.

PART-PART-WHOLE PROBLEMS

Part-Part-Whole problems involve static relationships among a particular set and its two disjoint subsets. Unlike the Join and Separate problems,

Unknown	Example
Result Unknown	Colleen had 8 guppies. She gave 3 guppies to Roger. How many guppies does Colleen have left?
Change Unknown	Colleen had 8 guppies. She gave some guppies to Roger. Then she had 5 guppies left. How many guppies did Colleen give Roger?
Start Unknown	Colleen had some guppies. She gave 3 guppies to Roger. Then she had 5 guppies left. How many guppies did Colleen have to start with?

FIGURE 2.2
Separate Problem Types

there is no direct or implied action, and there is no change over time. Because one set is not being joined to the other, both subsets assume equivalent roles in the problem. Therefore, only two Part-Part-Whole problem types exist. The problem either gives the two parts and asks one to find the size of the whole, or gives one of the parts and the whole and asks the solver to find the size of the other part (see Figure 2.3).

Unknown	Example
Whole Unknown	6 boys and 4 girls were playing soccer. How many children were playing soccer?
Part Unknown	10 children were playing soccer. 6 were boys and the rest were girls. How many girls were playing soccer?

FIGURE 2.3
Part-Part-Whole Problem Types

COMPARE PROBLEMS

Compare problems, like Part-Part-Whole problems, involve relationships between quantities rather than a joining or separating action, but Compare problems involve the comparison of two distinct, disjoint sets rather than the relationship between a set and its subsets. Because one set is compared to the other, one set is labeled the referent set and the other the compared set. The third entity in these problems is the difference, or the amount by which one set exceeds the other. The following comparison situation illustrates these different elements:

> *Mark has 3 mice.*   *Referent set*
> *Joy has 7 mice.*   *Compared set*
> *Joy has 4 more mice than Mark.*   *Difference*

In a Compare problem, any one of the three entities can be the unknown—the difference, the referent set, or the compared set. Figure 2.4 gives an example of each type of problem.

FIGURE 2.4
Compare Problem Types

Unknown	Example
Difference Unknown	Mark has 3 mice. Joy has 7 mice. Joy has how many more mice than Mark?
Compared Set Unknown	Mark has 3 mice. Joy has 4 more mice than Mark. How many mice does Joy have?
Referent Unknown	Joy has 7 mice. She has 4 more mice than Mark. How many mice does Mark have?

NUMBER SENTENCES: ANOTHER PERSPECTIVE ON PROBLEM TYPES

Another way to think about the distinctions among certain problem types is to consider number sentences that can be used to represent them. This is particularly useful with Join and Separate problems. The three terms in addition and subtraction number sentences, such as $5 + 2 = 7$ and $8 - 3 = 5$, correspond to the three quantities in Join and Separate problems. As with the word problems, any of the terms can be the unknown, yielding a number sentence that corresponds to a particular Join or Separate problem. In Figure 2.5, we present number sentences representing the word problems in Figures 2.1 and 2.2. These problems clearly illustrate the distinction between problems with different unknowns. It is not possible to make such a clear correspondence between each of the Part-Part-Whole or Compare problems and number sentences.

FIGURE 2.5
*Join/Separate Problems:
Number Sentence
Correspondence*

Unknown	Join	Separate
Result Unknown	$5 + 2 = \square$	$8 - 3 = \square$
Change Unknown	$5 + \square = 7$	$8 - \square = 5$
Start Unknown	$\square + 2 = 7$	$\square - 3 = 5$

OTHER CONSIDERATIONS

Children's ability to solve word problems depends to a great degree on their ability to recognize the distinctions among the problem types discussed in the preceding sections. Variations in the wording of the problems and the situations they depict can make a problem more or less difficult for children to solve.

We can make problems easier for children by making the action or relationships in the problems as clear as possible. For example, problems are easier if their wording corresponds to the action sequence. Compare the following problems:

Janice had 9 cookies. She ate 3 of them. How many cookies does Janice have left?

Janice just ate 3 cookies. She started with 9 cookies. How many cookies does Janice have now?

In the first problem, the starting quantity is given first. In the second problem, the change quantity is given before the starting quantity. This requires a more careful analysis of the problem. Consequently, the first problem tends to be easier, but the second problem provides a more rigorous test of whether children are carefully analyzing the problem or just mechanically operating on the numbers given in the problem.

Other changes in wording also help make the action sequence more apparent to children, although it is sometimes difficult to point to the factor that makes one problem easier than another. Join (Change Unknown) problems that ask "how many more are needed?" are generally easier than related problems in which the action has taken place in the past. For example, the first Join (Change Unknown) problem given below is easier for children than the second:

Tom has 3 stickers. How many more stickers does Tom have to get to have 8 stickers?

Tom had 3 stickers. His sister gave him some more stickers. Now he has 8 stickers. How many stickers did Tom's sister give him?

Another way that each of the problems described in the preceding sections can vary is whether or not the quantities described in the problems represent identifiable, discrete sets of objects. All of the problems presented in the preceding sections included quantities that could be directly represented using counters. Each counter could be used to represent a guppy or a mouse described in the problem. Such is not the case with problems involving continuous measures. For instance, consider this Join (Change Unknown) problem:

Cheryl's puppy weighed 3 pounds when she bought him. The puppy now weighs 12 pounds. How many pounds has the puppy gained?

The pounds of puppy are not clearly identifiable objects. Using counters to represent the twelve pounds of puppy involves a more abstract representation than the representation of mice or guppies.

SUMMARY

We have identified four basic classes of addition and subtraction word problems. By varying the unknown within each type, a total of eleven distinct types of problems can be constructed. In Figure 2.6, we present examples of each basic problem type. These eleven problems represent different interpretations of addition and subtraction. The different problem types within each of the four basic classes in Figure 2.6 contain the same key words, but the structure of each problem is unique and is related to how children solve the problems. We discuss the relationship between problem structure and children's solution strategies in the next chapter.

Problem Type			
Join	*(Result Unknown)* Connie had 5 marbles. Juan gave her 8 more marbles. How many marbles does Connie have altogether?	*(Change Unknown)* Connie has 5 marbles. How many more marbles does she need to have 13 marbles altogether?	*(Start Unknown)* Connie had some marbles. Juan gave her 5 more marbles. Now she has 13 marbles. How many marbles did Connie have to start with?
Separate	*(Result Unknown)* Connie had 13 marbles. She gave 5 to Juan. How many marbles does Connie have left?	*(Change Unknown)* Connie had 13 marbles. She gave some to Juan. Now she has 5 marbles left. How many marbles did Connie give to Juan?	*(Start Unknown)* Connie had some marbles. She gave 5 to Juan. Now she has 8 marbles left. How many marbles did Connie have to start with?
Part-Part-Whole	*(Whole Unknown)* Connie has 5 red marbles and 8 blue marbles. How many marbles does she have?	*(Part Unknown)* Connie has 13 marbles. 5 are red and the rest are blue. How many blue marbles does Connie have?	
Compare	*(Difference Unknown)* Connie has 13 marbles. Juan has 5 marbles. How many more marbles does Connie have than Juan?	*(Compare Quantity Unknown)* Juan has 5 marbles. Connie has 8 more than Juan. How many marbles does Connie have?	*(Referent Unknown)* Connie has 13 marbles. She has 5 more marbles than Juan. How many marbles does Juan have?

FIGURE 2.6   *Classification of Word Problems*

3 | ADDITION AND SUBTRACTION
Children's Solution Strategies

Research has identified a reasonably coherent picture of the strategies that children invent to solve addition and subtraction problems and how they evolve over time. The distinctions among problem types are reflected in children's solution processes. For the most basic strategies, children use physical objects (counters) or fingers to directly model the action or relationships described in each problem. Over time, children's strategies become more abstract and efficient. Direct Modeling strategies are replaced by more abstract Counting strategies, which in turn are replaced with number facts.

DIRECT MODELING STRATEGIES

Children invent Direct Modeling strategies to solve many of the problem types discussed earlier. To solve Join (Result Unknown) or Part-Part-Whole (Whole Unknown) problems, they use objects or fingers to represent each of the addends, and then they count the union of the two sets. We illustrate this strategy, called *Joining All*, in the following example:

> *Robin had 4 toy cars. Her friends gave her 7 more toy cars for her birthday. How many toy cars did she have then?*

> Karla makes a set of 4 cubes and a set of 7 cubes. She pushes them together and then counts them, "1, 2, 3, 4, 5, 6, 7, 8, 9, 10, 11," pointing to a cube with each count. Karla then responds, "She had 11 cars."

A similar strategy is used to solve Join (Change Unknown) problems. The primary difference is that the goal is to find the number of objects added to the initial set rather than the total. The child makes a set equivalent to the initial quantity and adds objects to it until the new collection is equal to the total given in the problem. The number of objects added is the answer. This strategy, called *Joining To*, is illustrated in the following example and in Figure 3.1:

> *Robin has 4 toy cars. How many more toy cars does she need to get for her birthday to have 11 toy cars all together?*

> Karla makes a set of 4 cubes. She adds additional cubes, counting, "5, 6, 7, 8, 9, 10, 11," until there is a total of 11 cubes. She keeps the cubes that she adds separate from the initial set of 4 cubes so that she can count them separately. She then counts the 7 cubes. Karla responds, "She needs 7 more."

One important difference between this strategy and the Joining All strategy is that children must somehow be able to distinguish the counters that they join to the initial set from the counters in the initial set so that they can count them separately. They may do this by keeping the counters physically separate or by using differently colored counters. This requires some advanced planning that the Joining All strategy does not.

The strategy that best models the Separate (Result Unknown) problem involves a subtracting or separating action. In this case, the larger quantity in the problem is initially represented, and the smaller quantity is subsequently removed from it. We give an example of this strategy, called *Separating From*, below:

> *Colleen had 12 guppies. She gave 5 guppies to Roger. How many guppies does Colleen have left?*

FIGURE 3.1
Using a Joining To Strategy to Solve a Join (Change Unknown) Problem

Karla makes a set of 12 cubes and removes 5 of them. She counts the remaining cubes. Karla then responds, "She has 7 left."

The Separate (Change Unknown) problem also involves a separating action. The strategy generally used to solve this problem is similar to the Separating From strategy except that objects are removed from the larger set until the number of objects remaining is equal to the smaller number given in the problem. The following example illustrates this strategy, called *Separating To*:

Roger had 13 stickers. He gave some to Colleen. He has 4 stickers left. How many stickers did he give to Colleen?

Karla makes a set of 13 cubes. She slowly removes cubes one by one, looking at the cubes remaining in the initial set. When she has removed 6 cubes, she counts the cubes in the remaining set. Finding that she has 7 cubes left, she removes 3 more cubes and again counts the cubes in the remaining set. Finding that there are now 4 cubes left, she stops removing cubes and counts the 9 cubes that were removed. Karla then responds, "He gave her 9."

Separating To involves a certain amount of trial and error because the child can't simply count objects as they are physically removed but must check the initial set to determine whether the appropriate number of objects remains. Children can most easily apply this strategy with small numbers so that the child can directly perceive whether there are two or three objects left.

Compare (Difference Unknown) problems describe a matching process. The strategy used to solve these problems involves the construction of a one-to-one correspondence between two sets until one set is exhausted. Counting the unmatched elements gives the answer. We illustrate the *Matching* strategy in the following example and in Figure 3.2 on page 18:

Mark has 6 mice. Joy has 11 mice. Joy has how many more mice than Mark?

Carl counts out a set of 6 cubes and another set of 11 cubes. He puts the set of 6 cubes in a row. He then makes a row of the 11 cubes next to the row of 6 cubes so that 6 of the cubes are aligned with the 6 cubes in the initial row. He then counts the 5 cubes that are not matched with a cube in the initial row. Carl responds, "She has 5 more."

It is difficult to model the Start Unknown problems because the initial quantity is unknown and therefore cannot be represented. A few children attempt to solve these problems using *Trial and Error*.

FIGURE 3.2
Using a Matching Strategy to Solve a Compare (Difference Unknown) Problem

The following example shows one such attempt:

Robin had some toy cars. Her friends gave her 5 more toy cars for her birthday. Then she had 11 toy cars. How many toy cars did Robin have before her birthday?

Karla counts out 3 cubes. She then adds 5 cubes to the original set and counts the total. Finding that the total is 8 rather than 11, she puts the cubes back with the unused cubes and starts over. Next she makes a set of 5 cubes and adds 5 more to it. Again she counts and realizes her original estimate is too low. This time she appears to recognize that she is only off by 1, so she adds 1 to her original set of 5 and then joins the other set of 5 to it. Counting the total, she finds that it is now 11. She recounts the first set of 6 cubes. She responds, "She had 6 before her birthday."

This example of Trial and Error illustrates a reasonably systematic attempt to solve the problem. When the first two estimates were too low, Karla increased them. Some children who attempt Trial and Error are less systematic.

Figure 3.3 summarizes the six Direct Modeling strategies described above.

COUNTING STRATEGIES

Counting strategies are more efficient and abstract than modeling with physical objects. In applying these strategies, a child recognizes that it is not

Problem	Strategy Description
Join (Result Unknown) Ellen had 3 tomatoes. She picked 5 more tomatoes. How many tomatoes does Ellen have now?	*Joining All* A set of 3 objects and a set of 5 objects are constructed. The sets are joined and the union of the two sets is counted.
Join (Change Unknown) Chuck had 3 peanuts. Clara gave him some more peanuts. Now Chuck has 8 peanuts. How many peanuts did Clara give him?	*Joining To* A set of 3 objects is constructed. Objects are added to this set until there is a total of 8 objects. The answer is found by counting the number of objects added.
Separate (Result Unknown) There were 8 seals playing. 3 seals swam away. How many seals were still playing?	*Separating From* A set of 8 objects is constructed. 3 objects are removed. The answer is the number of remaining objects.
Separate (Change Unknown) There were 8 people on the bus. Some people got off. Now there are 3 people on the bus. How many people got off the bus?	*Separating To* A set of 8 objects is counted out. Objects are removed from it until the number of objects remaining is equal to 3. The answer is the number of objects removed.
Compare (Difference Unknown) Megan has 3 stickers. Randy has 8 stickers. How many more stickers does Randy have than Megan?	*Matching* A set of 3 objects and a set of 8 objects are matched 1-to-1 until one set is used up. The answer is the number of unmatched objects remaining in the larger set.
Join (Start Unknown) Deborah had some books. She went to the library and got 3 more books. Now she has 8 books altogether. How many books did she have to start with?	*Trial and Error* A set of objects is constructed. A set of 3 objects is added to the set, and the resulting set is counted. If the final count is 8, then the number of objects in the initial set is the answer. If it is not 8, a different initial set is tried.

FIGURE 3.3
*Direct Modeling
Strategies*

necessary to physically construct and count the two sets described in a problem.

Children often use two related Counting strategies to solve Join (Result Unknown) and Part-Part-Whole (Whole Unknown) problems. With *Counting On From First*, a child begins counting forward from the first addend in the problem. The sequence ends when the number of counting steps that represents the second addend has been completed. The following example illustrates this strategy:

> *Robin had 4 toy cars. Her friends gave her 7 more toy cars for her birthday. How many toy cars did she have then?*

> Jamie counts, "4 [pause], 5, 6, 7, 8, 9, 10, 11. She has 11 cars." As Jamie counts, he extends a finger with each count. When he has extended seven fingers, he stops counting and gives the answer. (See Figure 3.4.)

The *Counting On From Larger* strategy is identical to the Counting On From First strategy except that the child begins counting with the larger of the two addends. George uses this strategy in response to the problem posed above.

> George counts, "7 [pause], 8, 9, 10, 11—11 toy cars." George also moves his fingers as he counts, but the movement is very slight, and it is easy to miss his use of them to keep track.

FIGURE 3.4
Using a Counting On From First Strategy to Solve a Join (Change Unknown) Problem

Note that in order to know when to stop counting, these two Counting strategies require some method of keeping track of the number of counting steps that represent the second addend. Most children use their fingers to keep track of the number of counts. A few may use counters or tallies, but a substantial number of children give no evidence of any physical action accompanying their counting. When counting is carried out mentally, it is difficult to determine how a child knows when to stop counting. Some children appear to use some sort of rhythmic or cadence counting such that counting words are clustered into groups of two or three. Others explicitly describe a double count (e.g., 6 is 1, 7 is 2, 8 is 3), but children generally have difficulty explaining this process.

When fingers or other objects are used in Counting strategies, they play a very different role than they do in Direct Modeling strategies. In this case, the fingers do not represent the second addend per se, but are used to keep track of the number of steps incremented in the counting sequence. When using fingers, children often do not appear to count their fingers; they recognize familiar finger patterns and can immediately tell when they have put up a given number of fingers.

A similar strategy is used to solve Join (Change Unknown) problems. Rather than the number reached being the answer, the answer is the number of steps in the counting sequence. The child initiates a forward counting strategy beginning with the smaller given number. The sequence ends with the larger given number. By keeping track of the number of counting words uttered in the sequence, the child determines the answer. This strategy, which is called *Counting On To*, is the counting analogue of the Direct Modeling strategy Joining To. The following example illustrates the Counting On To strategy:

> *Robin had 8 toy cars. Her parents gave her some more toy cars for her birthday. Then she had 13 toy cars. How many toy cars did her parents give her?*

> Ann counts, "8 [pause], 9, 10, 11, 12, 13." She extends a finger with each count as she says the sequence from 9 to 13. She looks at the extended fingers and responds, "They gave her 5."

Without counting, Ann could recognize that she had extended five fingers. Other children may have to actually count the extended fingers.

To reflect the action in the Separate (Result Unknown) problems, a backward counting sequence is employed. The child starts counting at the larger number given in the problem and counts backwards. This strategy, called *Counting Down*, is analogous to Separating From. Counting Down may take either of two forms:

> *Colleen had 11 guppies. She gave 3 guppies to Roger. How many guppies did she have left?*

Ann counts, "11, 10, 9 [pause], 8. She had 8 left." Ann uses her fingers to keep track of the number of steps in the counting sequence.

Bill counts, "11 [pause], 10, [raises one finger], 9 [raises a second finger], 8 [raises a third finger]. She had 8 left."

Ann says "11" as she mentally takes away the eleventh guppy, "10" as she takes away the tenth guppy, and "9" as she takes away the ninth guppy. The answer is the next (fourth) number in the backward sequence, 8. Bill's counting is different. As he takes one away, he says, "10," referring to the ten that remain and then "9" for the nine that remain. Finally, he says, "8" for the eight that remain as he removes the third guppy.

A backward counting sequence is also used to represent the action in a Separate (Change Unknown) problem. But the backward counting sequence in the *Counting Down To* strategy continues until the smaller number is reached; the number of words in the counting sequence is the solution to the problem. We illustrate this strategy, which is the counting counterpart of Separating To, below:

> *Colleen had 12 guppies. She gave some guppies to Roger. Then she had 8 guppies left. How many guppies did Colleen give to Roger?*

Ann counts, "12 [extends one finger], 11 [extends a second finger], 10 [extends a third finger], 9 [extends a fourth finger and pauses] 8." She does not extend a finger for the 8. She looks at the 4 extended fingers and answers, "She gave 4 to Roger."

Bill counts, "12 [pause], 11 [extends one finger], 10 [extends a second finger], 9 [extends a third finger], 8 [extends a fourth finger]." He looks at the 4 extended fingers and answers, "She gave 4 to Roger."

In Figure 3.5, we summarize the above Counting strategies.

DISTINCTION BETWEEN COUNTING AND MODELING STRATEGIES

It is important to note the distinction between Direct Modeling and Counting strategies. Direct Modeling is distinguished by the child's explicit physical representation of each quantity in a problem and the action or relationship involving those quantities before counting the resulting set. In using a Counting strategy, a child essentially recognizes that it is not necessary to actually construct and count sets. The answer can be figured out by focusing

Problem	Strategy Description
Join (Result Unknown) Ellen had 3 tomatoes. She picked 5 more tomatoes. How many tomatoes does she have now?	*Counting On From First* The counting sequence begins with 3 and continues on 5 more counts. The answer is the last number in the counting sequence.
Join (Result Unknown) Ellen had 3 tomatoes. She picked 5 more tomatoes. How many tomatoes does she have now?	*Counting On From Larger* The counting sequence begins with 5 and continues on 3 more counts. The answer is the last number in the counting sequence.
Join (Change Unknown) Chuck had 3 peanuts. Clara gave him some more peanuts. Now Chuck has 8 peanuts. How many peanuts did Clara give to him?	*Counting On To* A forward counting sequence starts from 3 and continues until 8 is reached. The answer is the number of counting words in the sequence.
Separate (Result Unknown) There were 8 seals playing. 3 seals swam away. How many seals were still playing?	*Counting Down* A backward counting sequence is initiated from 8. The sequence continues for 3 more counts. The last number in the counting sequence is the answer.
Separate (Change Unknown) There were 8 people on the bus. Some people got off. Now there are 3 people on the bus. How many people got off the bus?	*Counting Down To* A backward counting sequence starts from 8 and continues until 3 is reached. The answer is the number of words in the counting sequence.

FIGURE 3.5
Counting Strategies for Addition and Subtraction Problems

on the counting sequence itself. Counting strategies generally involve some sort of simultaneous double counting, and the physical objects a child may use (fingers, counters, tally marks) are used to keep track of counts rather than to represent objects in the problem.

Although children frequently use fingers with Counting strategies, the use of fingers does not distinguish Counting strategies from Direct Modeling strategies. As illustrated in the following examples (and shown in the photo at the beginning of Chapter 2), fingers may be used to directly model a problem or to keep track of the steps in a counting sequence:

> *Peter had 5 daisies. His sister gave him 3 more daisies. How many daisies did he have then?*

Angela directly models: She puts up 3 fingers on one hand and 5 fingers on the other hand. She then counts her fingers, bending one slightly with each count, "1, 2, 3, 4, 5, 6, 7, 8. He has 8 daisies."

Jerry uses his fingers in a counting strategy: He says, "5 [pause], 6, 7, 8," extending one finger for each count. "He has 8 daisies."

NUMBER FACTS

Children's solutions to word problems are not limited to Modeling and Counting strategies, as children do learn number facts both in and out of school and apply this knowledge to solve problems. Children learn certain number combinations before others, and they often use a small set of memorized facts to derive solutions for problems involving other number combinations. Children usually learn doubles (e.g., 4 + 4, 7 + 7) before other combinations, and they often learn sums of ten (e.g., 7 + 3, 4 + 6) relatively early. The following examples illustrate children's use of *Derived Facts:*

> *6 frogs were sitting on lily pads. 8 more frogs joined them. How many frogs were there then?*

Rudy, Denise, Theo, and Sandra each answer, "14," almost immediately.
Teacher: How do you know there were 14?
Rudy: Because 6 and 6 is 12, and 2 more is 14.
Denise: 8 and 8 is 16. But this is 8 and 6. That is 2 less, so it's 14.
Theo: Well, I took one from the 8 and gave it to the 6. That made 7 and 7, and that's 14.
Sandra: 8 and 2 more is 10, and 4 more is 14.

Derived Fact solutions are based on understanding relations between numbers, and it might be expected that they are used by only a handful of very bright students. This is not the case. Even without specific instruction, most children use Derived Facts before they have mastered all their number facts at a recall level. In a three-year longitudinal study of non-CGI classes, over 80 percent of the children used Derived Facts at some time in grades one through three, and Derived Facts represented the primary strategy of 40 percent of the children at some time during this period. In many CGI classes, most children use Derived Facts before they have learned all the number facts at a recall level. When children have the opportunity to discuss alternative strategies, the use of Derived Facts becomes even more prevalent.

Some children continue to use Counting strategies or Derived Facts for an extended period of time, and it should not be assumed that children recall facts simply because they appear to have recall of facts. Children can become very proficient in using Counting strategies and can apply them very quickly. Counting strategies and Derived Facts are relatively efficient strategies for solving problems. However, when given the opportunity to solve many problems with strategies they have invented, children eventually learn most number facts at a recall level.

RELATION OF STRATEGIES TO PROBLEM TYPES

We summarize the relation between strategies and problem types in Figure 3.6. Younger children generally select strategies that directly represent the action or relationships described in problems. For some problem types, the action dominates the problem more than others. Almost all children Join To

Problem Type	Direct Modeling	Counting
Join (Result Unknown) Part-Part-Whole (Whole Unknown)	Joining All	Counting On
Join (Change Unknown)	Joining To	Counting On To
Separate (Result Unknown)	Separating From	Counting Down
Separate (Change Unknown)	Separating To	Counting Down To
Compare (Difference Unknown)	Matching	**
Join (Start Unknown) Separate (Start Unknown)	Trial and Error	Trial and Error
Part-Part-Whole (Part Unknown)	**	**
Compare (Compared Quantity Unknown) Compare (Referent Unknown)	**	**

FIGURE 3.6
Relation of Strategy to Problem Types

*Note: ** indicates that there is not a commonly used strategy corresponding to the action or relationship described in the problem. For the Compare (Compared Quantity Unknown) problem, children usually use Joining All or Counting On strategies. For the other problems, children generally use Joining To, Separating From, Counting On To, or Counting Down.*

or Count On To to solve Join (Change Unknown) problems. Children consistently solve Separate (Result Unknown) problems with the Separating From strategy. Because it is relatively difficult to Count Down, some children use this strategy less frequently. As a consequence, some children who use Counting strategies that involve forward counting to solve other problems may continue to Separate From to solve Separate (Result Unknown) problems. Matching and Separating To are not used universally although most younger children use them. Children use Trial and Error even less frequently.

With experience in solving problems, children become more flexible in their selection of strategies so that they can select strategies that do not always correspond to the action in a given problem. However, even older children tend to select strategies that model the action or relationships for certain problems. Children generally model the very dominant action in a Separate (Change Unknown) or Join (Change Unknown) for an extended period of time. On the other hand, most older children replace the Matching strategy for Compare problems with one of the other common strategies that do not directly model the comparison relation described in Compare problems. As there is no counting analogue of Matching, children must select a strategy that does not model the Compare problem if they want to use a Counting strategy.

LEVELS OF DEVELOPMENT OF STRATEGIES

There is a great deal of variability in the ages at which children use different strategies. When they enter kindergarten, most children can solve some word problems using Direct Modeling strategies even when they have had little or no formal instruction in addition or subtraction. Some entering first-graders are able to use Counting strategies, and a few use Recall of Number Facts or Derived Facts consistently.

Most children pass through three levels in acquiring addition and subtraction problem-solving skills. Initially they solve problems exclusively by Direct Modeling. Over time, Direct Modeling strategies are replaced by the use of Counting strategies, and finally most children come to rely on number facts. The transition from Direct Modeling to using Counting strategies does not take place all at once, and for a time children may use both Direct Modeling and Counting strategies. Similarly, children learn a few number facts quite early, when they are still relying primarily on Direct Modeling or Counting strategies, and the use of recall and Derived Facts evolves over an extended period of time.

Direct Modeling Strategies

Initially, children are limited to Direct Modeling solutions. Direct modelers, however, are not uniformly successful in solving all problems that can be modeled because some problems are more difficult to model than others.

At first, young children are limited in their modeling capabilities. They do not plan ahead and can only think about one step at a time. This causes no problems with the Joining All and Separating From strategies, but it can cause difficulties in Joining To. Consider the following example:

Robin had 5 toy cars. How many more toy cars does she have to get for her birthday to make 9 toy cars?

Nick makes a set of 5 cubes and then adds 4 more cubes to the set counting, "6, 7, 8, 9," as he adds the cubes. He is not careful to keep the new cubes separate, so when he finishes adding them, he cannot distinguish them from the original set of 5 cubes. He looks confused for a moment and then counts the entire set of 9 cubes and responds, "9?"

Nick models the action in the problem, but he does not recognize that he needs to keep separate the four cubes that he adds on and the five cubes in the initial set. As a consequence, he has no way to figure out how many cubes he added. In other words, he simply modeled the action described in the problem without planning ahead how he was going to use his model to answer the question.

The only strategies available to children who only think about one step at a time are Joining All and Separating From. Therefore, they can only solve problems that can be modeled with these strategies: Join (Result Unknown), Part-Part-Whole (Whole Unknown), and Separate (Result Unknown) problems. With experience solving simple problems, children learn to reflect on their Modeling strategies. This gives them the ability to plan their solutions to avoid the errors illustrated in Nick's example above. Thus the ability to think about the entire problem—the question to be answered as well as the action in the problem—allows children to solve Join (Change Unknown) problems by Joining To.

Compare (Difference Unknown) problems may be slightly more difficult to model than Join (Change Unknown) problems. However, if the context or wording of the Compare problems provides cues for Matching, direct modelers can solve them. Graphing problems in which two quantities, like the number of boys and the number of girls in the class, are represented on a bar graph provide situations in which quantities can be compared. Children at this level quite readily solve such problems. The bar graph is a way of matching so that quantities can be compared in much the same way that the Matching strategy is applied to any Compare problem.

Most direct modelers have difficulty solving Start Unknown problems with understanding. Because the initial set is unknown, they cannot start out representing a given set. The only alternative for modeling the problem is Trial and Error, and Trial and Error is a difficult strategy for most direct modelers to apply. Direct modelers find the Part-Part-Whole (Part Unknown) problem difficult for a slightly different reason. Because there is no explicit action to represent, many of them have difficulty representing the problem with concrete objects. As a consequence, most direct modelers cannot solve this problem.

Counting Strategies

Gradually over a period of time, children replace concrete Direct Modeling strategies with more efficient Counting strategies, and the use of Counting strategies is an important marker in the development of number concepts. Counting strategies represent more than efficient procedures for calculating answers to addition and subtraction problems. They indicate a level of understanding of number concepts and an ability to reflect on numbers as abstract entities.

Initially, children may use both Direct Modeling and Counting strategies concurrently. At first, they use Counting strategies in situations in which they are particularly easy to apply, such as when the second addend is a small number or the first addend is relatively large:

> *Sam had 24 flowers. He picked 3 more. How many flowers did he have then?*

Even after children become quite comfortable with Counting strategies, they may occasionally fall back to Direct Modeling strategies with concrete objects. Most children come to rely on the Counting On strategies, but not all children use Counting Down consistently because of the difficulty in counting backwards.

Flexible Choice of Strategies

Initially, children use Counting strategies that are consistent with the action or relationships described in problems. In other words, the Counting strategies are abstractions of the corresponding Direct Modeling strategies they used previously. Over time, however, many children learn to represent problems with counting procedures that are not consistent with the structure of the problem. For example, they can solve Join (Start Unknown) problems by Counting On To, and they can solve Separate (Start Unknown) problems by Counting On. They also generally solve Compare (Difference Unknown) problems by either Counting Down or Counting On To, and some of them may even solve the Separate (Result Unknown) problems by Counting On To.

The development of understanding of part-whole relationships allows children to be more flexible in their choice of strategy. Children begin to learn that addition and subtraction problems can be thought of in terms of parts and wholes. In one large class of problems, the two parts are known, and the goal is to find the whole. In the other, one part and the whole are known, and the goal is to find the other part. All problems in which both parts are known can be solved by Joining All or Counting On. All problems in which one part and the whole are known can be solved using any one of several strategies, including Counting On To, Counting Down, Separating From, and so on. In this example, a child explains how she used part-whole relationships.

> *Some birds were sitting on a wire. 3 birds flew away. There were 8 birds still sitting on the wire. How many birds were sitting on the wire before the 3 birds flew away?*

Kisha: [Counts] 8 [pause], 9, 10, 11. There were 11.
Teacher: I understand how you found the answer, but how did you know to count on like that?
Kisha: Well, there were the 3 birds that flew away, and the 8 birds that were still sitting there. And I want to know how many there were all together. The 3 and the 8 together were how many birds there were on the wire. So I put them together. I counted on from 8 to get 11.

For the Join (Result Unknown), Separate (Start Unknown), and Part-Part-Whole (Whole Unknown) problems, both parts are known. For the Separate (Result and Change Unknown), the Join (Change and Start Unknown), and the Part-Part-Whole (Part Unknown) problems, the whole and one of the parts are unknown. Because Compare problems involve two disjoint sets, the part-whole scheme does not apply well to these problems. But at about the same time that children develop an understanding of part-whole, they are able to be flexible in their choice of strategy for this type of problem also.

Another basic principle that allows children to be more flexible in dealing with Join and Separate problems is an understanding that actions can be reversed. In other words, the act of joining objects to a set can be undone by removing the objects from the resulting set. For example, the following Start-Unknown problem can be solved by reversing the action:

> *Colleen had some stickers. She gave 3 stickers to Roger. She had 5 stickers left. How many stickers did Colleen have to start with?*

If the three stickers that were given away are put back with the five stickers that are left, the original set of stickers is restored. This analysis allows children to think of this problem in terms of a joining action so they can solve it without use of Trial and Error.

Number Facts

Even though Counting strategies can become very efficient, they are inefficient and distracting when dealing with very large numbers. Through experience solving problems, children begin to learn number facts so that they can recall them immediately. It is important to recognize, however, that number facts are learned at a recall level over a much longer period of time than previously has been assumed, and that many children may never learn all number facts at a recall level.

Children do not learn facts all at once, and they use selected number facts and Derived Facts at the direct modeling and counting levels. Although not all children use Derived Facts consistently, Derived Facts play an important role in solving problems and in learning number facts at a recall level. It is much easier for a child to learn to recall number facts if the child understands the relationships among number facts. Most children use Derived Facts for many combinations as they are learning number facts at a recall level, and it is important that all children at least understand relations among number facts (e.g., 6 + 7 is one more than 6 + 6), even if they do not use them consistently to derive other number facts.

INTEGRATION OF SOLUTION STRATEGIES AND PROBLEM TYPES

The relationships between strategies and problem types and the levels at which strategies may be used are represented in the Children's Solution Strategies chart (Figure 3.7). This figure presents a somewhat simplified version of what we have described above. Derived Facts and Recall of Number Facts are portrayed as cutting across all levels. Children use some number facts at all levels, and the use of number facts increases until number fact strategies become the dominant strategy.

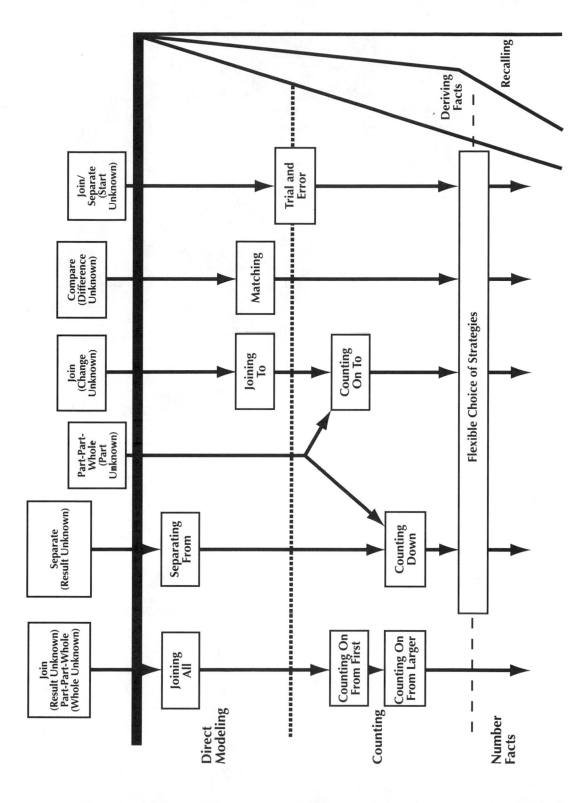

FIGURE 3.7 *Children's Solution Strategies*

4 | MULTIPLICATION AND DIVISION
Problem Types and Children's Solution Strategies

The analysis of addition and subtraction provides a framework that can be extended to multiplication and division. This chapter starts with a discussion of problem types that represent basic multiplication and division problems and the strategies that children generally use to solve them. These problems and strategies involve grouping or partitioning collections of countable objects. In the second part of the chapter, we examine some different problem types and the ways students may think about them.

GROUPING AND PARTITIONING PROBLEMS

Although not all real-life problems that can be solved by multiplication and division are grouped or partitioned into equivalent sets without remainders, the initial discussion of multiplication and division considers only those problems in which collections can be grouped or partitioned into equivalent groups with no remainders. Grouping and Partitioning problems all involve three quantities, as illustrated by the following example:

> *Megan has 5 bags of cookies. There are 3 cookies in each bag. All together she has 15 cookies.*

The three quantities in the problem are the number of bags, the number of cookies in each bag, and the total number of cookies. In a problem, any one of the three quantities can be unknown. When the total number of cookies Megan has all together is unknown, the problem is a *Multiplication* problem. When the number of groups or bags is unknown, the problem is called a *Measurement Division* problem. When the number of cookies in each bag or group is unknown, the problem is called a *Partitive Division* problem. The three problem types—Multiplication, Measurement Division, and Partitive Division—are illustrated in Figure 4.1.

Multiplication problems give the number of groups (the bags) and the number of objects in each group, and the unknown is the total number of

Multiplication	Megan has 5 bags of cookies. There are 3 cookies in each bag. How many cookies does Megan have all together?
Measurement Division	Megan has 15 cookies. She puts 3 cookies in each bag. How many bags can she fill?
Partitive Division	Megan has 15 cookies. She put the cookies into 5 bags with the same number of cookies in each bag. How many cookies are in each bag?

objects. Note that the two known numbers represent different things. One number represents the number of groups (bags), and one represents how many are in each group (the number of cookies in each bag). This distinction is important because it is reflected in the Modeling and Counting strategies that children use to solve the problem.

Measurement Division problems give the total number of objects and the number of objects in each group. The number of groups (the number of bags of cookies) is the unknown. Essentially, children use the number of objects in each group to measure the total number of objects, which is where the name *Measurement Division* comes from.

Partitive Division problems give the total number of objects and the number of groups, and the number of objects in each group (the number of cookies per bag) is unknown. Children partition the total number of objects into a given number of groups, hence the name *Partitive Division*. The distinctions between the Measurement and Partitive Division problems are critical because children initially solve them in very different ways, reflecting the different information given in the problem.

In summary, we have described three types of problems that represent multiplication and division. The three problem types are related but differ in what is known and what is unknown. In a Multiplication problem, the goal is to find the total number of objects. In a Measurement Division problem, the goal is to find the number of sets. In a Partitive Division problem, the goal is to find the number of objects in each set.

CHILDREN'S STRATEGIES FOR SOLVING MULTIPLICATION, MEASUREMENT DIVISION, AND PARTITIVE DIVISION PROBLEMS

As with addition and subtraction problems, children initially solve multiplication and division problems by directly modeling the action and relationships described in the problems. Over time, these Direct Modeling strategies are replaced by more efficient strategies based on counting, adding/subtracting, or the use of derived number facts.

Multiplication

Children first solve Multiplication problems by modeling each of the groups (using counters, tally marks, or other representations), and counting the total number of objects. This *Grouping* strategy is illustrated below and in Figure 4.2:

> *Ms. Jenkins bought 7 boxes of cupcakes. There were 4 cupcakes in each box. How many cupcakes did Ms. Jenkins buy?*

> Carla counts out one set of 4 blocks, then another set of 4 blocks, then a third set and a fourth set, a fifth, a sixth, and a seventh. After she has finished making 7 groups with 4 blocks in each set, she counts all the blocks and says, "28. She bought 28 cupcakes."

Measurement Division

Children initially solve Measurement Division problems by direct modeling. Children construct a given number of sets, each containing the specified number of objects. They then count how many sets they made. This strategy is called a *Measurement* strategy. There are at least two variations of the Measurement strategy, depending on whether the total number is counted first or later. The following examples and Figure 4.3 illustrate these variations:

> *There are 28 fish, with 7 fish in each fish bowl. How many fish bowls are there?*

FIGURE 4.2
Using a Grouping Strategy to Solve a Multiplication Problem

FIGURE 4.3
Using a Measurement Strategy to Solve a Measurement Division Problem

Geno counts out 28 linking cubes. He then connects them into groups of 7 and counts the groups. He says the answer is "4."

Maricela connects a group of 7 linking cubes, another group of 7, and a third group of 7. She then counts all the cubes in the 3 groups and finds there are only 21. She then counts out another group of 7 and counts all the cubes again. She now finds the total is 28, so she counts the groups and says, "4."

Both children made four sets with seven counters in each set. The difference between how Maricela and Geno solved this Measurement Division problem is that Geno first counted the twenty-eight counters and then separated them into groups of seven counters, whereas Maricela started by forming groups of seven until she had counted twenty-eight all together. The strategies are just variants of the same basic Measurement strategy, and it is not necessary to worry about which variation a child might be using. Both children directly represented the action described in the problem.

Partitive Division

Children also model Partitive Division problems directly by constructing groups of objects. The solution requires finding the number of objects in the group rather than the number of groups. There are several ways that a child might do this. One way is to deal the objects into the correct number of groups one at a time, until the total number of objects is used up. The following example illustrates this strategy:

> *Mr. Franke baked 20 cookies. He gave all the cookies to 4 friends, being careful to give the same number of cookies to each friend. How many cookies did each friend get?*

> Ellen counts out 20 counters. She places the counters into 4 separate places one at a time. After she puts one counter in each spot, she starts over and adds another counter to each set, continuing this process until she has used up all the counters. Then she counts the counters in one pile and says, "5 . . . each would get 5 cookies."

Many students do not systematically deal the counters out one by one. They start out putting more than one object in a group and then add or remove objects from each group as they find it necessary. In the following solution to the problem about Mr. Franke's cookies, a child uses this approach:

> Kang counts out 20 counters. He places 4 counters in one group, 4 in another group, 4 in another, and 4 in another until he sees that there are 4 groups. At this point he sees that he has not used up all the counters, so he adds 1 counter to each group. Then he counts the counters in one of the groups and answers, "5."

Although Kang put four counters in each group, his strategy for solving this Partitive Division problem was very different from the strategy used to solve a Measurement Division problem. Kang's initial goal was not to put four counters in each group; it was to construct four groups with the same number in each group and to use all of the counters. When he saw that he had not used up the counters, he added one to each group. He may have started with four in each group because that number was mentioned in the problem, but he was able to adjust the number of objects in each group.

Children sometimes start to solve a Partitive Division problem by putting too many objects in a group. For example, Kang might have guessed that each friend got six cookies and put six counters in each group. In that case, there would not have been enough counters to make the required number of groups, and he would have removed counters from each group to complete the last group.

Sometimes children attempt to represent the groups themselves with an object that is not part of the group. This allows the child to model the given number of groups before they begin to deal with the objects in the group. This may seem confusing, but most children do not have difficulty distinguishing between the object representing the group and the objects in the group when they use this strategy. The following solution to the same problem about Mr. Franke's twenty cookies illustrates this approach:

> First Rita counts out 20 counters. Then she selects 4 additional counters that are not part of the 20 to represent the 4 friends and puts them in separate places on the table. She deals the counters one by one to each of the 4 separate "friend's" places on the table.
>
> When she has used up all 20 counters, she counts the number of counters in one of the groups, not counting the single counter that she first put out to identify the group and answers, "5."
> *Teacher:* Good. I see how you got the 5, but can you tell me why you didn't count this [indicates the counter that represented the group]?
> *Rita:* That's one of the friends.

As they do with Measurement Division problems, some children may not count out the total set first, but keep track of it as they are placing the counters into groups. A child utilizes this approach to solve the problem below:

> *Linda had 12 cookies for the bake sale. She put them into 4 bags so that there were the same number of cookies in each bag. How many cookies were there in each bag?*

> Geri counts while she puts 4 counters in separate places on the table and says "1, 2, 3, 4." She then puts another counter by each of the first 4 counters and continues to count, "5, 6, 7, 8." She continues by adding another counter to each set and saying, "9, 10, 11, 12." She counts the counters in one set and says, "3."

These examples of strategies that children use for Partitive Division problems are just variations of the *Partitive* strategy. Basically, the Partitive strategy involves some form of directly modeling the action or relationships described in Partitive Division problems. A total number of objects are partitioned into a given number of sets, and the number of objects in one or more of the sets is counted to find the answer. Figure 4.4 contains a summary of the basic Direct Modeling strategies for Multiplication, Measurement Division, and Partitive Division problems.

Counting and Adding Strategies

As with addition and subtraction, children gradually replace Direct Modeling strategies with Counting strategies. However, it is more difficult to use Counting strategies for multiplication and division problems than it is for

Problem	Strategy Description
Multiplication Bart has 4 boxes of pencils. There are 6 pencils in each box. How many pencils does Bart have all together?	*Grouping* Make 4 groups with 6 counters in each group. Count all the counters to find the answer.
Measurement Division Bart has 24 pencils. They are packed 6 pencils to a box. How many boxes of pencils does he have?	*Measurement* Put 24 counters into groups with 6 counters in each group. Count the groups to find the answer.
Partitive Division Bart has 6 boxes of pencils with the same number of pencils in each box. All together he has 24 pencils. How many pencils are in each box?	*Partitive* Divide 24 counters into 6 groups with the same number of counters in each group. Count the counters in 1 group to find the answer.

FIGURE 4.4
Direct Modeling Strategies for Multiplication and Division Problems

addition and subtraction problems. As a result, children generally do not use Counting strategies as early for Grouping/Partitioning problems as they do for solving addition and subtraction problems.

Counting strategies used for Multiplication and Measurement Division problems often involve some form of skip-counting. The following is an example of a solution to a Grouping problem that involves skip-counting:

There are 3 tennis balls in a can. How many balls are there in 7 cans?

Linda: [Mumbles to herself, putting up fingers one at a time until she has put up seven fingers] 21—there are 21 balls.
Teacher: That's good, Linda. Can you tell me how you figured out that it was 21?
Linda: I counted 3, 6, 9, 12, 15, 18, 21. [With each count she extends a finger to keep track of the number of threes she has counted.]

Children generally are more proficient in skip-counting by certain numbers, like three and five, than they are by other numbers, such as seven. Also, some children are only proficient at skip-counting for the first three or four numbers in a sequence and need to complete their solutions by counting by ones. In this case they may use a combination of skip-counting and Counting On by One. The following example illustrates this strategy:

> *The teacher has 5 sheets of stickers. There are 4 stickers on each sheet. How many stickers does the teacher have?*

> Jeannie counts, "Let's see, 4, 8, 12, [pause] 13, 14, 15, 16, [pause] 17, 18, 19, 20—20 stickers."

Jeannie could count by four to twelve. After that she had to count on by ones, which she did in two segments. Note that children skip-count by the number of objects in each group, not by the number of groups. They keep track of the number of groups on their fingers or in some other way. This is a natural extension of the Direct Modeling strategy and corresponds to the way they count objects into groups when they directly model. Children do not easily recognize that they could skip-count by either number given in a Multiplication problem. For example, in the problem above, it might have been easier to skip-count by five, but that is not what Jeannie did, because there were four objects in the groups.

Many children also use addition strategies to solve Multiplication and Division problems. For example, rather than skip-counting, some children may repeatedly add the number representing the objects in each group. Skip-counting is essentially repeated addition, but some children tend to think of their solution more in terms of counting, and others think of it more in terms of adding. Addition strategies offer other ways to solve problems also. We illustrate a doubling approach in the following example:

> *A bottle of cola will fill 6 glasses. How many glasses can you fill with 7 bottles of cola?*

> Maria makes a drawing [Figure 4.5] and says, "42." [Keep in mind that the drawing is *Maria's* and represents her thinking. It is not an illustration used by a teacher.]
> *Teacher:* How did you do that?
> *Maria:* I added 6 plus 6 three times, added 12 plus 12, added another 12 to get 36, and then added the last 6 to get 42.

Counting Strategies for Measurement Division

Children use similar counting and addition and subtraction strategies to solve Measurement Division problems. The difference is that the children skip-count or add or subtract until they reach the given number. The answer is the number of times they have counted, added, or

FIGURE 4.5
*Presenting a Doubling
Strategy for a
Multiplication Problem*

subtracted, as shown in the following solution to a Measurement Division problem:

> *A restaurant puts 4 slices of cheese on each sandwich. How many sandwiches can they make with 24 pieces of cheese?*

> Susan counts, "Hmmm, 4, 8, 12, 16, 20, 24." With each count Susan extends one finger. When she is done counting, she looks at the six extended fingers and says, "6. They can make 6 sandwiches."

Note that, as with the counting example for the Multiplication problem above, Susan skip-counted the number of objects in each group. This fits the context of the Measurement Division problem.

Counting Strategies for Partitive Division

It is much more difficult to use strategies involving counting or adding to solve Partitive Division problems than it is for Multiplication and Measurement Division problems. For both the Multiplication and Measurement Division problems, children skip-count by the number of objects in each group. But for Partitive Division problems, the number of objects in each group is the unknown. Therefore, in order to use a Counting strategy that corresponds to the action or relationships in the problem, children may use Trial and Error to figure out which number to skip-count by or to add. They know the number of groups and the total number of objects. The number of groups tells them how many numbers there should be in the counting sequence, and the total number of objects tells them where the counting sequence should stop. The problem is to figure out what to count by (the number in each group). That is where Trial and Error comes in, as the following example illustrates:

> There are 24 children in the class. We want to divide the class into 6 teams with the same number of children on each team. How many children will there be on each team?

> Susan counts, "Let's see, 3, 6, 9, 12, 15, 18." With each count, Susan extends one finger. When she has extended 6 fingers, she pauses. "No, that's not big enough. Let's try 4. 4, 8, 12, 16, 20, 24." Again, Susan extends a finger with each count. When she reaches 24, she sees that there are 6 fingers extended. "That's it. There would be 4 in each group."

Essentially, Susan's problem was to find a number to count by, such that when there were six numbers in the counting sequence, the total would be twenty-four. She did not know what to count by, so she needed to guess. The first guess did not work. She had six fingers extended, indicating she had counted six times and she had not yet reached twenty-four. Consequently, she had to start over again with another number. She could see that three was too small, so she tried four. As this example illustrates, it is significantly more difficult to use a counting strategy for a Partitive Division problem than for a Multiplication or Measurement Division problem.

Derived Facts

As with addition and subtraction, children learn some multiplication facts before others. There are patterns for certain multiplication facts that make them especially easy to learn. For example, multiples of five and nine follow regular patterns. Children can use a core of known facts to derive other facts. Generally the Derived Facts involve a combination of known facts and addition or counting on. The known fact almost always involves one of the numbers given in the problem.

> There are 7 peaches in each box. How many peaches are there in 6 boxes?

> *Eliz:* [Almost immediately] 42.
> *Teacher:* That was quick. How did you figure that out so quickly?
> *Eliz:* Well, I know that 5 sevens is 35, so 1 more seven is just 42.

Children can relate division facts to the corresponding multiplication facts, and the strategies they use to derive division facts may be related to knowledge of multiplication facts.

There are 7 sticks of gum in a package. How many sticks of gum are there in 8 packages?

Eliz says, "Well, there would be 63 sticks of gum if it were 9 packages, but it's not 9, it's 8. So it has to be 7 less. Let's see, that's 60, 56. There are 56 pieces all together."

What to Do with What's Left Over

Because there are many situations in which the objects do not divide evenly without any leftovers, children need to deal with remainders. Children can solve problems with remainders by using the strategies already described, and problems with remainders are not a great deal more difficult than corresponding problems without remainders.

In solving problems with remainders, it is necessary to take into account how the remainder relates to the problem. The context of the problem generally dictates how the remainder is treated in answering the question. There are four basic ways this may occur. In the following Measurement Division problem, an extra car must be included for the two people left over:

20 people are going to a movie. 6 people can ride in each car. How many cars are needed to get all 20 people to the movie?

In each of the following Measurement and Partitive Division problems, the remainder is simply left over and is not taken into account:

It takes 3 eggs to make a cake. How many cakes can you make with 17 eggs?

Ms. Franke has 21 marbles. She wants to share them equally among her 5 children so that no one gets more than anyone else. How many marbles should she give to each child?

From the context of these problems, it is clear that only five cakes can be made and four marbles can be given to each child. The remainder is either ignored, or a child may suggest that the two eggs can be put back into the refrigerator and that Ms. Franke can keep the last marble.

A third possibility is that the remainder is the answer to the problem, as in the following Measurement and Partitive Division problems:

A store has 26 basketballs, which they want to pack in boxes so that there are 3 balls in each box. If they fill as many boxes as possible, how many balls will be left over?

Ms. Baker has 17 cupcakes. She wants to share them equally among her 3 daughters so that no one gets more than anyone else. If she gives each daughter as many cupcakes as possible, how many cupcakes will be left over for Ms. Baker to eat?

The fourth possibility is that the answer includes a fractional part. The following is an example of a Partitive Division problem in which a fraction is included in the answer:

Ms. Baker has 17 cupcakes. She wants to share them equally among her 3 children so that no one gets more than anyone else. She also wants to use all the cupcakes up. If she gives each child an equal amount, how many cupcakes will each child get?

MULTIPLICATION AND DIVISION WORD PROBLEMS IN THE PRIMARY GRADES

There are good reasons for introducing multiplication and division word problems early in the mathematics curriculum. With experience, many kindergarten children can solve simple multiplication and division problems by using counters to model the groups described in the problems. By first and second grade, many children use a variety of strategies to solve multiplication and division word problems. Thus, children throughout the primary grades can solve multiplication and division word problems. Integrating the problems into the primary curriculum provides children a basis for learning formal multiplication and division concepts as well as expanding their opportunities to solve problems in a variety of contexts.

Multiplication and division problems also provide children the opportunity to develop a broad understanding of some of the fundamental grouping ideas underlying place value. In order to learn base-ten concepts with understanding, children must understand the concepts that underlie multiplication and division. In fact, many base-ten problems are essentially multiplication or division problems involving groups of ten. For example, the problem "How many tens are there in 73?" is a Measurement Division problem. A common activity for introducing base-ten number concepts is to count collections of objects by organizing them into groups of ten. There is a direct parallel between this counting procedure and the strategy children use to solve a Measurement Division problem involving groups of ten. The problems presented in Figure 4.6 illustrate how fundamental base-ten number concepts are related to multiplication and division problems.

When children have experiences with multiplication and division problems before they encounter base-ten concepts, they have the opportunity to develop an understanding of basic principles that are essential to understand base-ten numbers. As they learn base-ten principles, they only have to deal with the special characteristics of grouping by ten and how such groupings

Grouping (No Extra)	Write the number.	Carla has 3 boxes of crayons. There are 10 crayons in each box. How many crayons does Carla have all together?
Grouping (Extra)	Write the number.	Mel has 2 boxes of crayons. There are 10 crayons in each box. He also has 4 extra crayons. How many crayons does he have in all?
Measurement Division	Circle groups of 10 and write the number. How many tens are there in 32?	Josh has 32 Ping Pong balls. He wants to put them in boxes that hold 10 Ping Pong balls. How many boxes can he fill? How many balls are left over?

are related to the names assigned to them. Thus, providing children the opportunity to solve a variety of multiplication and division problems can provide a context for them to develop a rich understanding of mathematics in a way that is meaningful to them.

OTHER MULTIPLICATION AND DIVISION PROBLEMS

The multiplication and division problems discussed up to this point have dealt with grouping and partitioning collections of discrete objects that can be counted. There are related problems that involve Rates and Multiplicative Comparisons rather than collections of countable objects. These problems are similar in structure to the multiplication and division problems we have presented so far in that they also involve Multiplication, Partitive Division, and Measurement Division situations. For other problems this is not the case. Problems involving Areas, Arrays, or Combinations have completely different structures.

Related Problems: Rate, Price, and Multiplicative Comparison Problems

Rate Problems

Rate problems do not necessarily have countable groups, but they do have quantities in them that children can represent with counters. These problems may be somewhat more difficult for children than are problems involving countable groups of objects, but they are not out of reach of young children. Consider the following problems, which illustrate Multiplication, Measurement Division, and Partitive Division rate problems, respectively:

> *A baby elephant gains 4 pounds each day. How many pounds will the baby elephant gain in 8 days?*

> *A baby elephant gains 4 pounds each day. How many days will it take the baby elephant to gain 32 pounds?*

> *A baby elephant gained 32 pounds in 8 days. If she gained the same amount of weight each day, how much did she gain in one day?*

These problems are not exactly like Grouping and Partitioning problems because they each involve a rate rather than a number of objects. In each case the rate is pounds per day. Although the eight days are not really eight groups, and the four and thirty-two pounds are not countable objects, the problems do have some similarities to the basic Grouping and Partitioning problems and can be thought of in much the same way. A child can think about how much the elephant gains in one day, in two days, and so forth. So the first problem might be solved by making eight groups of counters with four counters in each group. Each group of four counters would represent how much the baby elephant gained each day, and the total number of counters would represent the total weight gained.

The second problem could be solved by counting out thirty-two counters and removing sets of four and counting the number of sets removed to determine how many days it would take to gain thirty-two pounds. The last problem could be solved by distributing the thirty-two counters into eight piles, which represent the days, and counting the objects in each pile to determine how much the elephant gained daily. Thus, even though the problems do not describe actions involving discrete sets, children can solve them in much the same way that they solve the Grouping and Partitioning problems.

The following are some other common situations involving rate:

How many miles does a bicycle travel in 3 hours at an average speed of 12 miles per hour?

A baby sitter earns 3 dollars per hour for baby-sitting. How many hours will he have to baby-sit to earn 18 dollars?

Price Problems

Price problems are a special kind of Rate problem in which the rate is a price per item. Children generally are familiar with money and solve Price problems quite easily using the same strategies that they use for basic Grouping and Partitioning problems. The following problems illustrate the three basic Grouping and Partitioning problems in a price context. The first problem is a Multiplication problem, the second is a Measurement Division problem, and the third is a Partitive Division problem.

How much would 5 pieces of bubble gum cost if each piece costs 4 cents?

Bubble gum costs 4 cents for each piece. How many pieces of bubble gum can you buy with 20 cents?

If you can buy 5 pieces of bubble gum with 20 cents, how much does each piece cost?

Multiplicative Comparison Problems

In all the problems described to this point, all of the numbers represent some sort of quantity: the number of groups, the number of objects in a group, the total number of objects, the price, the rate, and so forth. For Multiplicative Comparison, this is not the case. Multiplicative Comparison problems involve a comparison of two quantities in which one is described as a multiple of the other. The relation between quantities is described in terms of how many times larger one is than the other. The number quantifying this relationship is not an identifiable quantity. In the following problem, the animals' weights are measurable quantities, but the other quantity (three times as much) simply describes the relation between the measurable quantities:

The first-grade class has a hamster and a gerbil. The hamster weighs 3 times as much as the gerbil. The gerbil weighs 9 ounces. How much does the hamster weigh?

Multiplicative Comparison problems also can be constructed for any of the three basic problem types, as illustrated in Figure 4.7. To solve Multiplicative

Problem Type	Multiplication	Measurement Division	Partitive Division
Grouping/ Partitioning	Gene has 4 tomato plants. There are 6 tomatoes on each plant. How many tomatoes are there all together?	Gene has some tomato plants. There are 6 tomatoes on each plant. All together there are 24 tomatoes. How many tomato plants does Gene have?	Gene has 4 tomato plants. There are the same number of tomatoes on each plant. All together there are 20 tomatoes. How many tomatoes are there on each tomato plant?
Rate	Ellen walks 3 miles an hour. How many miles does she walk in 5 hours?	Ellen walks 3 miles an hour. How many hours will it take her to walk 15 miles?	Ellen walked 15 miles. It took her 5 hours. If she walked the same speed the whole way, how far did she walk in one hour?
Price	Pies cost 4 dollars each. How much do 7 pies cost?	Pies cost 4 dollars each. How many pies can you buy for $28?	Jan bought 7 pies. He spent a total of $28. If each pie cost the same amount, how much did one pie cost?
Multiplicative Comparison	The giraffe in the zoo is 3 times as tall as the kangaroo. The kangaroo is 6 feet tall. How tall is the giraffe?	The giraffe is 18 feet tall. The kangaroo is 6 feet tall. The giraffe is how many times taller than the kangaroo?	The giraffe is 18 feet tall. She is 3 times as tall as the kangaroo. How tall is the kangaroo?

FIGURE 4.7   *Grouping/Partitioning, Rate, Price, and Multiplicative Comparison Problems*

Comparison problems, children must understand the meaning of such terms as "six times as many." Grouping and Rate problems do not use this terminology.

Common Features

The differences among all of these problems can be relatively minor, and it is not necessary to be concerned about whether a problem falls in one particular class or another. The critical differences are between Multiplication, Measurement Division, and Partitive Division problems. It is the differences among these three basic types that are reflected in children's thinking.

We have introduced Rate, Price, and Multiplicative Comparison problems because it is important to provide opportunities for children to solve a variety of problems involving different kinds of quantities. Whereas the basic multiplication and division problems involve only whole numbers, Rate, Price, and Multiplicative Comparison problems can be extended to include multiplication and division of fractions. Consider the problems about the baby elephant and its weight gain. It could have gained $3/4$ pound each day or $3\frac{1}{2}$ pounds, and the time period could have been $1/2$ day or 7.25 days. Thus, including these problems with whole numbers in the primary grades lays the groundwork for developing an understanding of multiplication and division of fractions in later grades.

Symmetric Problems: Area, Array, and Combination Problems

One important characteristic of all problem types discussed previously is that they are not symmetric, that is, the numbers in them are related to specific referents, and the referents are not interchangeable. When a problem talks about five bags of cookies with seven cookies in each bag, young children initially think about the five in relation to the number of bags and the seven in relation to the number of cookies in each bag. They solve the problem by making five groups with seven objects in each group. It is not obvious to most young children that they also could solve the problem by making seven groups with five objects in each group, or that they could count by fives.

At some point, children need to learn that $5 \times 7 = 7 \times 5$, but it is important to recognize that young children do not immediately understand that the two numbers in the Multiplication problems discussed above can be interchanged or that the methods used to solve a Measurement Division problem also can be applied to a Partitive Division problem. There are multiplication and division problems, however, in which the factors play equivalent roles. We call these problems symmetric. Area and Array problems and Combination problems are types of Symmetric problems.

Area and Array Problems

One important application of multiplication is calculating the area of a rectangular region by multiplying the length of the region by the width. This involves a very different conception of multiplication than has been discussed so far in this chapter. Unlike the Grouping/Partitioning, Rate, and Multiplicative Comparison problems, the two factors in an Area problem do not have distinctly different roles and are not attached to a specific referent. Although the longest side of a rectangle is frequently called the length and the shorter side the width, the length and width play essentially the same role in calculating the area of a rectangle.

Thus, Area problems represent a new type of multiplication and division problem. Because the two factors in an Area problem are interchangeable, there are not two distinct types of Area division problems. In other words, because the length and width play equivalent roles in area problems, it does not matter whether the length or the width is unknown.[*] The following are examples of each basic type of Area problem:

> *A farmer plants a rectangular vegetable garden that measures 6 meters along one side and 8 meters along an adjacent side. How many square meters of garden did the farmer plant?*

> *A farmer plans to plant a rectangular vegetable garden. She has enough room to make the garden 6 meters along one side. How long does she have to make the adjacent side in order to have 48 square meters of garden?*

There is more to developing area concepts than multiplying the dimensions of a rectangle to calculate the area, but children can solve problems that introduce multiplication and division in area contexts before they have developed a complete understanding of area concepts. The following example is a problem that might be solved by modeling before children have developed a formal notion of area:

> *A baker has a pan of fudge that measures 8 inches on one side and 9 inches on another side. If the fudge is cut into square pieces 1 inch on a side, how many pieces of fudge does the pan hold?*

Children might model this problem by drawing a picture of the pan divided into seventy-two squares. They may count each of the squares, or they may find a more efficient way to figure out the number of pieces, like adding nine eight times or doubling (9, 18, 36, 72). In these solutions children need to construct some representation of the problem in order to solve it. In other problems, children might work directly with rectangular regions partitioned into square units. For example, they might find the number of floor tiles covering the floor of the classroom or work from a picture of a rectangular region partitioned into identical units.

Finding the number of items in a rectangular array involves the same basic conception of multiplication as finding the area of a rectangle. The primary difference is that arrays may be made up of discrete objects (cookies on a cookie sheet, rows of chairs, etc.). Array problems can be directly modeled in a systematic way by constructing a given number of rows of counters with the same number of counters in each row. Children may interpret some problems

---

[*]Recall that a comparable situation holds for Part-Part-Whole (Part Unknown) problems, which we discussed in Chapter 2. Although there are three distinct Join problems and three Separate problems, there are only two Part-Part-Whole problems. There is no distinction between the parts, so it does not matter which part is the unknown.

as either Array or Grouping problems. For example, the following problem could be thought of as an array of chairs or as groups of chairs in each row:

For the second-grade play, the chairs have been put into 4 rows with 4 chairs in each row. How many chairs have been put out for the play?

Some children might solve this problem by arranging counters into a four-by-four array (see Figure 4.8), whereas others may just make four groups of four.

Although arrays provide natural representations for some types of multiplication and division problems, young children do not normally construct arrays unless a problem calls for them. Many textbooks use pictures of arrays to represent a wide variety of multiplication or division situations, including situations that children would not naturally represent as arrays. For example, in some texts a Grouping problem such as the following might be accompanied by a picture of an array with four rows of peanuts with three peanuts in each row:

How many peanuts would the monkey eat if she ate 4 groups of peanuts with 3 peanuts in each group?

In this case, a Grouping problem, which children usually think of as a certain number of groups with the same number in each group, has been

FIGURE 4.8
Using an Array to Solve a Multiplication Problem

represented as an array. This is not an incorrect representation of the problem, but it is not the form that young children generally use to model it. Textbook authors often use arrays because they provide a context for developing the principle that multiplication is commutative (3 x 5 = 5 x 3). But children do not naturally construct an array for a Multiplication problem unless an array is specifically described in the problem.

Thus, Array and Area problems provide a very different context for developing multiplication and division concepts than Grouping/Partitioning problems do. Furthermore, they illustrate important concepts that are not easily related to Grouping/Partitioning problems. Array problems can be used to help children understand that multiplication is commutative, and Area problems provide a basis for developing an understanding of multiplication and division of fractions.

Combination Problems

Another type of Symmetric problem involves different combinations that can be constructed from given sets of objects, as this example does:

> *The Friendly Old Ice Cream Shop has 3 types of ice cream cones. They also have 4 flavors of ice cream. How many different combinations of an ice cream flavor and cone type can you get at the Friendly Old Ice Cream Shop?*

This problem is symmetric because the cones and the ice cream flavors can be interchanged in thinking about the problem. There is no real difference in thinking of the problem in terms of the number of flavors that go with each cone or in terms of the number of cones that go with each flavor. The problem might be solved by identifying three types of cones (sugar cones, waffle cones, and wafer cones) and four flavors (blue moon, bubble gum, double chocolate, licorice) and actually making all the combinations (blue moon on a sugar cone, blue moon on a waffle cone, etc.). Many young children have difficulty constructing all the combinations in this way. They often are not systematic and only construct a few of the combinations. For example, they may concentrate on using each type of cone once, or they may not be systematic in constructing the combinations and then not recognize that they do not have them all. On the other hand, some children may recognize that it is not necessary to actually make all the combinations. They may see that for each cone, there will be four flavors, and be able to think of the problem as three groups of four. Alternatively, they might see that for each flavor there will be three cones and relate the problem to four groups of three.

Combination problems are not as central to developing concepts of multiplication and division in the primary grades as the other problems that we have discussed in this chapter. Because of their difficulty, they might be used sparingly in the primary grades. They do, however, present a different type of challenging problem that can lead to a good discussion of strategies. Even though some children may have difficulty systematically organizing their combinations, the discussion may help children begin to see the need to organize results in systematic ways.

5 | PROBLEM SOLVING AS MODELING

The unifying theme of the analyses of children's mathematical thinking is that children naturally attempt to model the action or relationships in problems. They first directly model the situations or relationships with physical objects. They then move on to various Counting strategies in which the actions or relationships are at first somewhat visible but become less visible as children's thinking matures. Thus, children's solution strategies are first fairly exact models of problem action or relationships. As thinking progresses to using more Counting strategies, their representation becomes more abstract. Counting and Direct Modeling strategies are simply specific instances of the fundamental principle of modeling, and it is helpful to think of them as attempts to model problems rather than as a collection of distinct strategies. Over time, children begin to use fact-based strategies that are even more abstract and do not necessarily reflect problem structure.

The conception of problem solving as modeling not only serves as a basis for understanding children's strategies for solving addition, subtraction, multiplication, and division problems; it also can provide a unifying framework for thinking about problem solving in the primary grades. It may seem obvious that children would attempt to perform the action in a problem if they have no other way to solve it. Many older children, however, appear to approach word problems by looking for superficial clues like using the operation that has just been taught, deciding what operation to use based on the numbers in the problem, or looking for key words to decide whether to add, subtract, multiply, or divide. In other words, many students seem to abandon a fundamentally sound and powerful general problem-solving approach for the mechanical application of arithmetic skills.

If older children simply applied some of the intuitive, analytic modeling skills exhibited by young children to analyze problem situations, it appears that they would avoid some of their most glaring problem-solving errors. A fundamental issue is how to help children build upon and extend the intuitive modeling skills that they apply to basic problems as young children. That is a primary goal of Cognitively Guided Instruction.

Although the foregoing analysis focuses on basic addition, subtraction, multiplication, and division situations, the general principle that children model the action and relations in problems applies to more complex problem situations as well. Many problem situations that are appropriate for elementary school children involve combinations of the problems described in the preceding chapters, and children's methods for solving them can be understood in light of the strategies that children use to solve one-step problems. For example, consider the following problem:

Maggie had 3 packages of cupcakes. There were 4 cupcakes in each package. She ate 5 cupcakes. How many cupcakes were left?

This problem is a combination of Multiplication and Separate (Result Unknown) problems, and young children readily solve it using a combination of the strategies used to solve these two types of problems. A typical solution would be first to count out three groups of counters with four counters in each group and then remove five counters.

Children can solve a variety of other problems by modeling, such as this example:

19 children are taking a minibus to the zoo. They will have to sit either 2 or 3 to a seat. The bus has 7 seats. How many children will have to sit 3 to a seat and how many can sit 2 to a seat?

To solve this problem, young children typically set out nineteen counters and attempt to place them in seven groups of either two or three to a group until the counters are used up. Some children use trial and error to place the counters in groups, and others systematically deal the counters into seven groups until the counters are used up. Note that, even though the groups the children create to solve this problem will not have the same number of counters and the answer is not the number of counters in a given group, the strategies used are similar to those used to solve a Partitive Division problem. The key to understanding children's solutions to these problems lies in noting that children model the problem situations directly.

Thinking of children's problem solving as modeling also provides some perspective on whether a given problem might be difficult for children. When children have difficulty, even with a problem that appears relatively simple to us (e.g., a one-step Join [Start Unknown] problem), it is often because they cannot figure out how to model it. The examples above illustrate that children can solve even seemingly complex problems as long as the action or relationships in a problem can be modeled in a reasonably straightforward fashion. Because modeling provides a framework in which problem solving becomes a meaning-making activity, a focus on problem solving as modeling may do more than just provide children with a general strategy for solving problems. It seems likely that such a focus will also have an impact on children's conceptions of problem solving and of themselves as problem solvers. If from an early age, children are taught to approach problem solving as a way of making sense out of problem situations, they may come to believe that learning and doing mathematics involves the solution of problems in ways that are always meaningful.

This conception of problem solving provides a foundation for integrating instruction in problem solving with instruction in fundamental mathematical concepts and skills. Problem solving becomes a basis for learning symbols and formal procedures. Not only can symbols and procedures be presented as ways of representing problem situations, but the construction of procedures for calculating answers can be presented as a problem-solving task. These themes are developed in greater detail in the next chapter.

6 | MULTIDIGIT NUMBER CONCEPTS

The central principle that children must grasp to understand base-ten numbers is that collections of ten (or one hundred or one thousand) can be counted. (For simplicity, we describe the basic grouping and naming principles for two-digit numbers.) This means that we can talk about the number of tens (or one hundreds or one thousands) just as we talk about the number of individual units. For example, a collection of thirty-six counters can be thought about as thirty-six individual counters or as three groups of ten counters and six additional counters. To find out how many objects are in a group, a child can count all of the objects by ones or put the objects in groups of ten and count the groups of ten and the leftover objects.

PROBLEM CONTEXTS FOR GROUPING BY TEN

The fundamental context for developing this notion of grouping by ten is found in the Multiplication and Measurement Division situations discussed in Chapter 4. We give specific examples of Grouping and Partitioning Problems in Figure 4.4. What is unique about problems that develop base-ten ideas is that objects are collected into groups of ten. That allows children to use principles of the base-ten number system to solve them.

Both Multiplication and Measurement Division problems provide contexts for introducing base-ten concepts that provide a link with the problems children have solved with smaller numbers. Partitive Division problems, on the other hand, are not particularly good problems to introduce concepts of grouping by ten. With Partitive Division problems, the number of objects in each group is the unknown. The basic idea of place value involves grouping with ten in each group. The number in the group is given.

Posing Word Problems

As noted above, Multiplication and Measurement Division word problems provide contexts for fundamental base-ten concepts involving grouping by ten. For example, consider children's responses to the following Multiplication problem:

> *Our class has 5 boxes of doughnuts. There are 10 doughnuts in each box. We also have 3 extra doughnuts. How many doughnuts do we have all together?*

Robin counts out 5 groups of individual counters with 10 counters in each group. He then adds 3 more counters and counts the entire set of 53 counters by ones.

Anna uses linking cubes to solve the problem. These are separate cubes that can be joined together. In this case, the teacher made sure that the cubes were always stored with ten cubes linked so that children could use them when solving problems involving two-digit numbers. Anna has worked with the cubes previously and knows that there are 10 cubes in each rod. She puts out 5 ten-rods and then 3 loose cubes. She counts up along one of the rods, "1, 2, 3, 4, 5, 6, 7, 8, 9, 10 [picks up the next rod and continues counting the individual cubes] 11, 12 . . ." She continues counting the individual cubes in each rod. When she is finished counting all the individual cubes in the 5 rods, she continues the count with the loose cubes, "51, 52, 53. There are 53 cubes all together."

Bob also puts out 5 ten-rods and 3 loose cubes, but he counts each of the ten-rods by 10 rather than by 1: "10, 20, 30, 40, 50, 51, 52, 53."

Tanya gives a response that is similar to Bob's, but she does not use any materials: "Let's see. That's 10, 20, 30, 40, 50 [putting up a finger with each count], 51, 52, 53 [again keeping track of the ones on her fingers]. We have 53."

Julio immediately answered, "53. Well, there's 5 boxes of 10 doughnuts. 5 tens is 50, and the 3 more doughnuts make 53."

Robin and Anna both counted by ones. Anna knew that there were ten cubes in each rod, but she was unable to use this information to find the total number of cubes. Bob, on the other hand, was able to count the groups of ten. His response was similar to Tanya's except that Tanya did not have to actually construct the sets. Sometimes children use cubes when they are available even though they do not need to. Bob might have been able to give a response similar to Tanya's if the materials were not available. On the other hand, some children do need the support of the physical material.

Measurement Division problems involving groups of ten provide another context for engaging in discussion of grouping concepts. Here are the same five children's responses to the following Measurement Division problem:

Jim picked 54 flowers. He put them into bunches with 10 flowers in each bunch. How many bunches of flowers did Jim make?

Robin and Anna count out 54 counters. They make groups with 10 counters in each group and count the number of groups, "5."

Bob puts out 5 ten-rods to represent the 50 flowers and 4 counters to represent the 4 extra flowers. He looks at the collection for a moment, and then counts the ten-rods, "5."

Tanya counts by 10, "10, 20, 30, 40, 50." With each count, she extends a finger. When she reaches 50, she sees that she has raised 5 fingers and responds, "5."

Julio immediately responds, "5, because there are 5 tens in 54."

These responses demonstrate the same progression of understanding of base-ten numbers as the responses to the multiplication problems described above.

Problems in which there are more than ten individual units require an additional measure of flexibility in thinking about multidigit numbers. Consider the following example:

The other first-grade class has 4 boxes of doughnuts with 10 doughnuts in each box, and they also have 17 individual doughnuts. How many doughnuts do they have all together?

Bob puts out 4 ten-rods and 17 cubes. He counts the ten-rods and cubes, "10, 20, 30, 40, 41, 42, 43, . . . 55, 56, 57."

Misha goes through the same counting sequence as Bob, but she does not use any counters. As she counts from 10 to 40 by 10, she puts up 4 fingers. When she reaches 40, she puts down her fingers so that she can use them to keep track as she counts on 17 from 40. As she counts from 40 to 50, she puts up a finger with each count. At 50, she puts them down again so that she can use them to keep track as she counts on 7 more from 50.

Julio says, "Well, that's 40, and then 10 more is 50, then 7 is 57."

Bob and Misha solved the problem successfully, but they were not very flexible in their thinking. They did not recognize that seventeen could be thought of as ten and seven more so that the ten could be combined with the other four tens. Instead they used the more laborious process of Counting

On By One. Julio was more flexible in his response. He understood that different groupings of ten are possible. Fifty-seven can be thought of as five tens and seven ones, as four tens and seventeen ones, or even as two tens and thirty-seven ones. This understanding represents an important milestone in the development of base-ten number concepts.

Using Objects Grouped by Ten

Children can also learn about base-ten concepts by working directly with objects grouped by ten. As might be expected, children's strategies are similar to the strategies they use for word problems involving groups of ten. The following examples illustrate the different strategies children might use to solve a problem in which objects are grouped by ten:

> [Teacher puts out 3 loose popsicle sticks and 5 bundles of popsicle sticks held together with a rubber band.] Each of these bundles has the same number of popsicle sticks in it. There are 10 popsicle sticks in each of these bundles. Do you want to count the sticks in one of the bundles to be sure that there are 10? . . . Okay, so there are 10 sticks in each bundle. Can you tell me how many popsicle sticks there are all together counting all the sticks? [Sweeps her hand over the entire collection of 5 bundles and 3 loose sticks.]

> Robin takes apart 1 of the bundles and counts all of the individual sticks, "1, 2, 3, 4, 5, 6, 7, 8, 9, 10 [takes apart the next bundle and continues counting the individual sticks], 11, 12, . . ." Robin continues counting the individual sticks in each bundle. When he is finished counting all the loose sticks in the 5 bundles, he continues the count with the individual sticks, "51, 52, 53. There are 53 popsicle sticks all together."

> Tanya points to each bundle as she counts, "Let's see. That's 10, 20, 30, 40, 50, [pointing to the loose sticks] 51, 52, 53. There's 53."

> Julio immediately answers, "Fifty-three." When asked how he knows that, he says, "Well, I can see the 5 tens, that's 50, and the 3 more make 53."

Robin counted the sticks one by one. He could count above fifty, so it is likely that he could solve problems involving quite large numbers by counting by ones, but he did not appear to understand that he could count groups of ten directly. He probably recognizes some repeated patterns in the string of number words that he uses to count, but the groups of ten appear to carry no significance with regard to the number assigned to the collection of counters.

Both Tanya and Julio counted collections of ten. Tanya actually counted by tens and then continued Counting On by ones. Julio immediately recognized that five groups of ten was fifty and that three more was fifty-three. His response is perhaps a little more advanced than Tanya's, but many children count by tens when they are perfectly capable of counting the tens as Julio did.

The distinction between counting by ones and using base-ten number concepts is further illustrated in the following exchange during which the teacher extended the above problem:

[After each child gives the answer 53, the teacher adds 1 more bundle of 10 sticks to the collection.] Watch what I do. I'm putting 10 more here. Now how many are here all together? [Indicates the collection of sticks with a sweep of her hand.]

Robin: [Counting on by ones] Mmm, 53 [pause], 54, 55, 56, 57, 58, 59, 60, 61, 62, 63 [extending a finger with each count until 10 fingers are extended]. There are 63.
Tanya: [Recounting all the tens and then the ones] 10, 20, 30, 40, 50, 60, 61, 62, 63.
Julio: [Immediately] 63. That's just 10 more than 53.
Teacher: Okay, but how did you know that it was 63?
Julio: Well, you see 53 has 5 tens, and you put one more ten, that's 6 tens. That's 60, and then there's the 3. That's 63.

Again Robin demonstrated no understanding that collections of ten could be counted directly. Although Tanya used base-ten concepts, her knowledge does not seem to be as flexible as Julio's. She did not appear to recognize immediately what effect adding a ten had on the number of sticks. She had to re-count all the tens rather than just incrementing her previous answer by ten.

We give a summary of children's strategies for problems that elicit basic concepts of grouping by ten in Figure 6.1 (see page 64).

CHILDREN'S STRATEGIES FOR SOLVING MULTIDIGIT PROBLEMS

Algorithms, or formal procedures for computing answers to multidigit addition/subtraction problems, depend upon base-ten number concepts. In the past it has been assumed that this means that it is necessary to develop base-ten number concepts before children can add, subtract, multiply, and divide two- and three-digit numbers. That assumption has not proven valid. As long as children can count, they can solve problems involving two-digit numbers even when they have limited notions of grouping by ten.

Problem	Strategies		
	Counting by Ones	*Counting by Tens*	*Direct Place Value*
Multiplication John has 6 pages of stickers. There are 10 stickers on each page. He also has 4 more stickers. How many stickers does he have in all?	Makes 6 groups of counters with 10 counters in each group. Adds 4 additional counters and counts the set by ones.	Counts, "10, 20, 30, 40, 50, 60, 61, 62, 63, 64," keeping track on fingers.	Says, "64. 6 tens is 60 and 4 more is 64."
Measurement Division Mary has 64 stickers. She pastes them in her sticker book so that there are 10 stickers on each page. How many pages can she fill?	Counts out 64 counters and puts them into groups with 10 in each group. Counts the number of groups.	Counts, "10, 20, 30, 40, 50, 60," putting up a finger with each count. Counts fingers to get answer of 6.	Says, "6. There are 6 tens in 60."

FIGURE 6.1   *Problems That Elicit Grouping by Ten Strategies*

Problems with two- and three-digit numbers actually provide a context for children to develop an understanding of base-ten numbers.

We are not suggesting that children should be taught formal computational algorithms before they understand base-ten numbers. We are suggesting, however, that children who do not have a complete understanding of base-ten numbers can construct solutions to multidigit problems that are meaningful to them. As they talk about alternative solutions to these problems and develop increasingly efficient ways to solve them, their understanding of base-ten numbers increases concurrently with an understanding of how to apply this knowledge to solve problems. Children acquire the skills and concepts required to solve problems as they are solving them, and their understanding of underlying base-ten concepts increases as well.

Addition and Subtraction

There are direct parallels between the strategies children use for multidigit problems and the strategies they use for problems with smaller numbers. Children use counters to directly model the action in problems, and they invent mental strategies that essentially are abstractions of these Modeling strategies.

Counting Single Units

Before looking at strategies that use base-ten number concepts, consider the following example, which illustrates how children solve problems involving two-digit numbers without using base-ten number concepts.

> *Misha has 34 dollars. How many dollars does she have to earn to have 47 dollars?*

Kang counts out a set of 34 counters. He continues counting out counters, "35, 36, 37, . . . ," until he has put out a total of 47 counters. He keeps the counters put out after the first 34 in a separate pile, which he now counts, "1, 2, 3, . . . 13. She needs 13 more."

Sue Ellen puts out a ten-rod and says, "Ten." She puts out another ten-rod, but she counts the individual cubes starting with 11, "11, 12, 13 . . . 20." She puts out another ten-rod and again counts the individual cubes, "21, 22, 23, . . . 30." Then she puts out 4 individual cubes, counting on, "31, 32, 33, 34." Then she counts on from 34 as she puts out individual cubes into a separate pile, "35, 36, 37, . . . 47." Next she counts the cubes in the second pile and announces that the answer is 13.

Fateen counts on from 34 to 47, "34 [pause], 35, 36, . . . 46, 47." With each count after 34, he extends a finger. When he has used up 10 fingers, he puts them all down and starts extending them again.
Fateen: Thirteen dollars.
Teacher: Can you tell me how you did that?
Fateen: I counted 34, 35, 36 . . .
Teacher: Okay. But how did you know that it was 13?
Fateen: I kept track on my fingers.
Teacher: But you don't have 13 fingers.
Fateen: No, but see after I put up 10, I started over again, there were 3 more: 11, 12, 13.

Kang's solution was identical to a strategy that he might have used with small numbers. All that was required was the ability to count up to forty-seven objects.

Sue Ellen's strategy was essentially the same as Kang's. She used ten-rods, but she counted each of the cubes by ones. The ten-rods merely served as a way of keeping the counters together. She clearly knew that there were ten cubes in each rod, as she did not count the cubes in the first rod. But she was not able to count the collections of tens.

Fateen Counted On To by ones. Because Fateen ran out of fingers to keep track with, his solution required a little more sophistication, but it essentially is just a variant of Counting On To by ones. This solution, although more difficult than Kang's or Sue Ellen's, made only limited use of base-ten number concepts.

Direct Modeling with Tens

The following solutions illustrate how children use knowledge of base-ten together with the direct modeling strategies they use for addition/subtraction problems. For these problems, the children had either a collection of base-ten blocks or linking cubes. The base-ten blocks consist of one-centimeter cubes and rods that are ten-centimeters long, with each centimeter marked off (see Figure 6.2).

> *There were 28 girls and 35 boys on the playground at recess. How many children were there on the playground at recess?*

Ralph uses the base-ten blocks. He puts out 2 ten-rods and 8 blocks. In another pile, he puts 3 ten-rods and 5 blocks. He pushes the bars and blocks together and counts all the individual blocks by one, "1, 2, 3, 4, 5, 6, 7, 8, 9, 10, 11, . . . 59, 60, 61, 62, 63."

Misha also uses the base-ten blocks as shown in Figure 6.2. She puts out 2 ten-rods and 8 blocks. In another pile she puts 3 ten-rods and 5 blocks. She pushes the bars and blocks together and first counts the ten-bars. Then she starts to count the blocks. When she has counted 10 blocks, she pauses a moment and then lines the 10 blocks up together so that they look like a ten-rod. Then she counts the rest of the single blocks, "1, 2, 3." Finally she counts the ten-rods again including the ten-rod that she has made, "There were 63 children."

Ralph was just beginning to develop an understanding of base-ten concepts, and his knowledge appeared to be tenuous. He could construct sets using groups of ten, but when it came to finding how many there were all together, he reverted to counting by ones. Misha, on the other hand, used groupings of ten both to construct the sets and to find the total.

Problems involving a Separating From strategy can be somewhat more difficult, depending on the materials available. Consider the following solutions to a Separate (Result Unknown) problem:

> *There were 51 geese in the farmer's field. 28 of the geese flew away. How many geese were left in the field?*

Steve uses the linking cubes. He puts out 5 ten-rods and 1 extra cube. He takes away 2 ten-rods. Then he breaks 8 cubes off 1 of the ten-rods. He puts the remaining 2 cubes with the extra cube. He looks at the pile of ten-rods and cubes that are left and says, "23."

Misha uses the base-ten rods. She puts out 5 ten-rods and 1 extra cube. First she takes away 2 ten-rods. Then she takes away 1 ten-rod and replaces it with 10 cubes from the original pile. Now there are 11 cubes in the pile. She removes 8 of them. She counts the 2 ten-rods remaining and the 3 blocks and says, "23."

Steve's solution was a relatively straightforward extension of the Separating From strategy used with smaller numbers. He used knowledge of groupings of ten both to construct the initial set and to remove twenty-eight blocks, but his solution did not require any knowledge of trading tens for ones. Misha's solution, on the other hand, did involve trading tens for ones. Because she could not break her ten-rod up into individual units, she traded it for ten cubes so that she could take eight away. This required the additional knowledge that fifty-one can be represented as five tens and one unit or as four tens and eleven ones.

The use of base-ten blocks does not necessarily force children to trade tens for ones. Some children simply cover up some of the blocks on a ten-rod with one of their fingers. On the other hand, it is not necessary for children to physically trade a ten-rod for ten ones to understand that one ten is the same as ten ones and use that knowledge in solving the problem. Look at how two children solved the same problem:

There were 51 geese in the farmer's field. 28 of the geese flew away. How many geese were left in the field?

FIGURE 6.2
Modeling a Part-Part-Whole (Whole Unknown) Problem with Tens

Ralph makes a set of 5 ten-rods and 1 cube. He takes away 2 ten-rods, and looks at the remaining blocks for a long time.
Teacher: What's the matter?
Ralph: I can't take away the 8.
Teacher: Is there anything you could do so that you could take away 8?
Ralph: I don't know . . . [Eventually he pushes the base-10 blocks back and uses single counters to solve the problem.]

Pedro puts out 5 ten-rods and 1 cube, then removes 2 ten-rods. He says, "Well, if I take 8 from one of those tens, I will have 2 left. Those 2 together with the 1 make 3, so that's 2 tens and 3—23.

Ralph did not seem to understand that he could break one of the tens up into ten ones, so he could not use base-ten materials to solve the problem. Pedro did not physically trade a ten-rod for ten ones, but he knew that each of the ten-rods could be broken up into ten cubes. He could use the principle that one ten is equal to ten ones to solve the problem. He did not have to make the actual trade with the blocks. This is an important point. It is not children's manipulations of materials that is important; it is their understanding of the principles involved in the manipulations.

The knowledge demonstrated by Pedro and by Misha represents a reasonably substantial step in learning base-ten number concepts. Many children can construct and count sets using knowledge of groupings of ten before they understand that within a particular representation of a number the tens can be broken apart. As a consequence, Join (Result Unknown) problems may be somewhat easier for some children than Separate (Result Unknown) problems, depending on the strategy they attempt to use. Note that Misha's solution to the addition problem did not require her to actually trade ones for tens.

Children's solutions of Join (Change Unknown) problems shows the same combination of Direct Modeling and use of knowledge of base-ten concepts found for Join (Result Unknown) and Separate (Result Unknown) problems, but Join (Change Unknown) problems can present additional difficulties when multidigit numbers are involved. The examples below illustrate one successful attempt and one unsuccessful attempt to model the action in a Join (Change Unknown) problem.

Elisa has 37 dollars. How many more dollars does she have to earn to have 53 dollars?

Steve puts out 3 ten-rods and 7 cubes. He then puts a ten-rod in a separate pile and says, "That's forty-seven." Then he puts loose cubes with the ten-rod counting, "48, 49, 50, 51, 52, 53." Then he counts the loose cubes and says, "That's 6 and 10 more—that's 16."

James had 39 stickers. He got some more stickers for his birthday. Then he had 61 stickers. How many stickers did James get for his birthday?

Diana puts out 3 ten-rods made of linking cubes. She takes another rod and breaks one cube off it and puts the nine-rod with the 3 ten-rods. She hesitates a moment and then puts 2 more ten-rods with the others, keeping them a little apart. Then she gets another cube and after a moment puts it on the nine-rod to make it a ten-rod. Then she adds another cube to the collection. Now she has 61 cubes all together (6 ten-rods and 1 loose cube); but because she connected the loose cube to make a complete ten-rod, she cannot tell which cubes were in the original set of 39 and which cubes she added on to get to 61. She stares at the collection for a long time and is clearly confused. Ultimately, she guesses at an answer.

Diana had two conflicting goals in solving this problem. She wanted to join cubes together to make tens, and she needed to keep the cubes representing the stickers James got for his birthday separate from the original set of thirty-nine cubes. This difficulty does not come up with smaller numbers.

The above problems all involve two-digit numbers, but children's ability to use materials to solve problems is not limited to two-digit numbers. The solution shown in Figure 6.3 illustrates how one first-grader solved this problem involving three-digit numbers:

The elephant had 407 peanuts. She ate 129 of them. How many peanuts did the elephant have left?

FIGURE 6.3
Modeling a Separate (Result Unknown) Problem with Hundreds, Tens, and Ones

Sue draws four large squares and below them seven tallies. Then she crosses out one large square saying, "Okay, that's the 100. Now I need to take away 20." She crosses out another big square and draws 10 small circles below the squares. Then she crosses out 2 of the circles, "Okay, now the 9." She crosses out the 7 tallies. She hesitates a moment, then crosses out another circle and draws 10 tallies below the other tallies. She crosses out 2 of those tallies. Then she counts the circles and the tallies and says, "278."

Because this problem involved both tens and hundreds, Sue needed some way to represent both tens and hundreds. She drew large squares to represent hundreds and circles to represent tens. She started subtracting with the hundreds and then subtracted the tens. She also started to remove ones before she recognized that she had to trade a ten for ten ones.

Invented Algorithms

Based on their experience modeling problems with base-ten materials, children can invent their own algorithms for adding and subtracting without the blocks. Invented algorithms differ from standard written algorithms in an important way. Children often carry out invented algorithms in their heads rather than on paper, and they report them using spoken number words. The explanations children give for their invented algorithms tend to rely on properties of spoken number words, where the tens, hundreds, and so on, are specifically labeled. In some cases, the algorithms children invent are quite similar to the standard algorithms traditionally taught in school; others are quite different. The invented algorithms share common elements with the Derived Fact solutions that children use with smaller numbers. In both cases children demonstrate flexibility in thinking about numbers, as numbers are broken apart and put together in different ways.

One basic type of invented algorithm involves successively incrementing or decreasing partial sums or differences. With the other major type of invented algorithm, the tens and ones are operated on separately, and the results subsequently combined. Combining the tens and ones separately is more closely related to the procedures used in the standard addition and subtraction algorithms than to the procedures in successive incrementing. The following examples illustrate the *Incrementing* strategies that children use for Join (Result Unknown) and Part-Part-Whole (Whole Unknown) situations. The same Incrementing and Combining Tens and Ones strategies are used for purely computational problems like 35 + 27.

There were 27 boys and 35 girls on the playground at recess. How many children were on the playground at recess?

Todd: Let's see. 20 and 30, that's 50, and 7 more is 57. Then the 5. 57 and 3 is 60, and the 2 more from the 5 is 62. There were 62.

Kisha: 20 [pause], 30, 40, 50 [pause], 57, 58, 59, 60, 61, 62. There were 62.

Both Todd and Kisha used an Incrementing strategy in which they successively added on each of the parts to the partial sum. Each of them used a different method of finding each of the partial sums. Kisha Counted On, and Todd used Recall of Number Facts and Derived Facts. Contrast these solutions with the following solutions based on a *Combining Tens and Ones* strategy:

There were 58 geese and 37 ducks in the marsh. How many birds were in the marsh?

Linda: 50 and 30, that's 80. Then 8 and 7, that's, ahh, 9, 10, 11, 12, 13, 14, 15. So it's 80 and 15 more. That's 90, 95. There were 95.

Juan: 5 and 3 is 8, that's 80. Then the 8 and the 7 . . . um, 7 and 7 is 14, so 8 and 7 is 15. Okay, so now 15 and 80 is 95.

Notice that both children combined the tens and ones separately. They started with the tens' place and subsequently adjusted their answers when they included the ten from the ones' place. Both children also thought about the numbers in the tens' place as multiples of ten (fifty and thirty, not five and three as is done in the standard paper-and-pencil algorithm). Juan added five and three, but he immediately recognized that he had eighty rather than just eight.

Some children use a combination of Incrementing and Combining Tens and Ones, particularly when they are combining two three-digit numbers. Below is an example of how Ellen constructed a solution to a problem involving three digits:

There were 246 stalks of corn in a row. The farmer planted 178 more stalks of corn in the row. How many stalks of corn were there in the row then?

Ellen: Well, 2 plus 1 is 3, so I know it's 200 and 100, so now it's somewhere in the 300s. And then you have to add the tens on. And the tens are 4 and 7. . . well, um, if you started at 70, 80, 90, 100. Right? And that's 4 hundreds because of that [100 + 300] . . . But you've still got one more ten. So if you're doing it 300 plus 40 plus 70, you'd have 4 hundreds and 1 ten. But you're not doing that. So what you need to do then is add 6 more onto 10, which is 16. And then 8 more—17, 18, 19, 20, 21, 22, 23, 24. So that's 124—I mean 424.

Children generally have more difficulty with Separate (Result Unknown) problems. As a consequence, many children, even those able to invent algorithms in other problems, use base-ten materials to solve Separate (Result Unknown) problems. In spite of the difficulties, however, children do invent strategies for solving these problems, as illustrated by the following examples:

> *Gary had 73 dollars. He spent 55 dollars on a pet snake. How many dollars did Gary have left?*
>
> *Kisha:* Mmm, 73 take away 50. That's 23. Now the 5. Take away 3. That's 20, and take away the other 2—that's 18. He had 18.

Kisha records and shares her strategy using the notation illustrated in Figure 6.4.

> *Todd:* 70 take away 50 is 20, and 5 from the 20, that's 15. Then I have the 3 more from the 73, so that's 18.

Both Kisha and Todd used an Incrementing strategy, similar to the Incrementing strategy they used in the problems described on pages 70–71. A comparison of Todd's solutions to these problems illustrates why Separate (Result Unknown) problems are more difficult. For his solution to the Part-Part-Whole (Whole Unknown) problem, everything was added. For the Separate (Result Unknown) problem, there were two actions: the three from the seventy-three had to be added to the partial sum and the five taken away. Because there is more to keep track of when using an Incrementing strategy for a Separate (Result Unknown) problem, children frequently get mixed up (e.g., take away the three also). In spite of the difficulties in using an Incremental strategy to subtract, this strategy is easier than subtracting

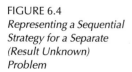

FIGURE 6.4
Representing a Sequential Strategy for a Separate (Result Unknown) Problem

by Combining Tens and Ones for most children. Although most children use an Incrementing strategy to subtract, some children do use a Combining Tens and Ones strategy as the following example illustrates.

> *Gary had 73 dollars. He spent 55 dollars on a pet snake. How many dollars did Gary have left?*

> *Linda:* The 70 take away the 50, that's 20. So now take the 5 from the 3. Hmmm, that's 2, so I need to take those 2 from the 20. So that's 18.

Linda subtracted the tens and then the ones. She could not actually take five away from three, so she took the three away from the five. The most common error that children make with subtraction problems starts out this same way. Children who do not understand subtraction frequently subtract the smaller number from the larger in each column. For example, for 345–168, they would get 223. Linda recognized, however, that she needed to take the two away from the twenty to solve the problem.

Children who are flexible in choosing strategies for different problems might recognize that they do not have to use a separating strategy for this problem. It can also be solved using an additive strategy that is usually used for Join (Change Unknown) problems. The following is another solution to the above problem:

> *Andy:* Well, 55 and 10 more is 65, and 5 more than that is 70, and 3 more is 73. So I had 10 and 5 and 3, that's 18.

Children most readily invent strategies for solving Join (Change Unknown) problems using some version of an Incrementing strategy. Here are several variations of Incrementing strategies for a Join (Change Unknown) problem:

> *Misha has 37 dollars. How many more dollars does she have to earn to have 61 dollars to buy a dog?*

> *Ricardo:* Mmm, 37, 47, 57, 67. No, that's too much. 37, 47, 57. That's 20. Now, ahh, 58, 59, 60, 61 [extends a finger with each count from 58 to 61]. 24. She has to earn 24 dollars.

> *Megan:* 37 [pause] 38, 39, 40 [extends three fingers as she counts from 38 to 40] 50, 60, 61 [extends another finger]. That's 24; 24 dollars.

Ricardo and Megan used slightly different ways to increment. Riccardo counted on by tens first and then counted on by ones to get the answer. Megan counted on by ones to get to a decade, counted by tens from the decade, and finished counting by ones.

Invented Algorithms for Special Number Combinations

Children also invent algorithms for certain problems based on special characteristics of the number combinations in the problems. One number might be adjusted up or down to the nearest ten or hundred with corresponding adjustments made in the other number.

> *The lion cub weighs 98 pounds. How much will she weigh when she gains 56 more pounds?*

> *Todd:* 98 and 56. If I make 98 into 100, I need to take 2 from the 56. So this is like 100 plus 54. So it's 154.

These strategies, which are called *Compensating* strategies because one number is adjusted to compensate for changes in the other number, are very similar to the Derived Fact strategies that children use for adding and subtracting small numbers. In both cases the numbers are adjusted to make the calculation easier. Examples of the three major types of invented strategies are presented in Figure 6.5.

Problem	Incrementing	Combining Tens and Ones	Compensating
Join (Result Unknown) Paul had 28 strawberries in his basket. He picked 35 more strawberries. How many strawberries did he have then?	"20 and 30 is 50, and 8 more is 58. 2 more is 60, and 3 more than that is 63."	"20 and 30 is 50. 8 plus 5 is like 8 plus 2 and 3 more, so it's 13. 50 and 13 is 63."	"30 and 35 would be 65. But it's 28, so it's 2 less. It's 63."
Separate (Result Unknown) Paul had 75 strawberries in his basket. He ate 26. How many did he have left?	"70 take away 20 is 50, and take away 6 more is 44. But you have to put back the 5 from the 75. That's 49."	"70 take away 20 is 50. 5 take away 6, that makes 1 more to take away from the 50. That's 49."	"If it was 75 take away 25, it would be 50. But it's 26, so you have to take one more away. 49."
Join (Change Unknown) Paul has 47 strawberries in his basket. How many more strawberries does he have to pick to have 75 all together?	"47 and 3 is 50 and 20 more is 70. So that's 23, but I need 5 more, so it's 28." "47, 57, 67. That's 20. 67 and 3 is 70, and 5 more is 75. So 8 and the 20, 28."	*Combining Tens and Ones is not commonly used for Join (Change Unknown).*	"If it were 45, it would be 30. But it's 47, so it's 2 less. 28."

FIGURE 6.5 *Invented Algorithms*

Benefits of Inventing Algorithms

When children invent their own algorithms, they often avoid some of the more serious misconceptions that children exhibit when they try to imitate symbolic manipulations that someone else shows them. This is not to say that children's invented algorithms are always correct, but when children invent algorithms for themselves, they have some basis for understanding and correcting their errors.

The standard written algorithms have evolved over centuries to be efficient methods for calculation. But the efficiency comes at a cost. The algorithms are not very transparent: It is not clear why they work. Children's invented algorithms are based directly on their understanding of base-ten grouping concepts. They are not isolated procedures. Children talk about combining fifty and thirty or five tens and three tens, rather than adding numbers in the same column. What may be lost in efficiency is more than made up in the fact that invented algorithms are more conceptual and consequently less likely to foster serious misconceptions and errors.

The following example illustrates how invented algorithms can help children avoid some serious errors:

> *There were 302 animals at the zoo. 104 of the animals were monkeys. How many animals were not monkeys?*
>
> *Todd:* Well, if I take away the 100, that's 202. 4 less than that is like 2 less than 200. That's 198.

Problems with zeros are notoriously difficult for children using standard written algorithms, but they pose no special problem for children like Todd who use an invented algorithm.

Furthermore, children become quite proficient in using invented algorithms, and there is not a huge difference in the time it takes children to use invented algorithms and the time it takes them to solve the same problem with a standard algorithm. Invented algorithms actually can be more efficient than standard written algorithms. The above examples with the zeros and the Compensating strategy are both easier and more efficient than the standard written algorithms applied to the same problems.

The use of invented algorithms also can contribute to the development of children's number sense and estimation abilities. Invented algorithms require that children think about the size of numbers and that they break numbers apart in different ways. Because children generally start adding the larger digits first, estimation strategies are a natural extension of invented algorithms.

Finally, the use of invented algorithms can contribute to children's understanding of fundamental base-ten concepts, as invented algorithms consistently require children to think about base-ten grouping concepts in different contexts. Furthermore, listening to children describe their invented algorithms provides teachers with insight about what children actually understand about base-ten numbers and multidigit computation. Children talk about their invented strategies in terms of their conceptual knowledge of base-ten principles.

Multiplication and Division

The development of multiplication and division strategies for multidigit numbers follows the same general pattern as the development of addition and subtraction strategies, but there are some added twists. Children may initially use individual counters to solve multidigit problems if the numbers are not too large. In order to use base-ten materials to solve a wide range of multidigit multiplication and division problems, children need to be relatively flexible in understanding that tens can be broken apart. For example, if children do not understand that forty-two can be represented with three tens and twelve ones as well as with four tens and two ones, they have difficulty using base-ten materials to solve a Partitive Division problem in which forty-two objects are distributed among three groups. Children's invented algorithms for multiplication and division generally build on their procedures for adding and subtracting multidigit numbers.

Modeling with Base-Ten Materials

Multiplication Children's use of base-ten materials to solve Multiplication problems is a relatively straightforward extension of the grouping strategy they use for smaller numbers.

> *The school bought 6 boxes of markers. There are 24 markers in each box. How many markers are there all together?*

> Mary makes 6 groups of markers with 2 ten-rods and 4 blocks in each group. She pushes them together, and starts putting blocks into rows of 10. When she has made 2 rows of 10, there are 4 blocks left. She then counts all the ten-rods together with the 2 tens that she has constructed, "1, 2, 3, 4, . . .11, 12, 13, 14. That's 140, and 4 more is 144."

As with problems involving smaller numbers, children tend to represent the number of groups and the number of objects in a group directly. Mary made six groups to represent the six boxes, and she put twenty-four in each group to represent the number of markers in each box. If the problem had stated that there were twenty-four boxes with six markers in each box, it is likely that she would have made twenty-four sets with six counters in each set. In this case she probably would have just counted the total set of markers one by one and would not have used base-ten materials to represent the problem. Children tend to use base-ten materials to solve a multiplication problem only when more than ten objects are in the collections described in the problem.

Measurement Division Children also use base-ten materials when a problem calls for organizing objects into groups with more than ten objects in each group. For many Measurement and Partitive Division problems, it is necessary to break tens apart (or trade tens for ones) to form the groups. We illustrate how one child did this to solve the Measurement Division problem below:

> *The class baked 84 cookies. We want to put them into boxes to sell at the school bake sale. If we put 12 cookies into each box, how many boxes can we fill?*

> Mary gets out 8 ten-rods and 4 blocks. She makes 2 groups with 1 ten-rod and 2 blocks in each group. She trades a ten-rod for 10 blocks and makes 5 more groups, with a ten-rod and 2 blocks in each group. She then counts the groups, "7."

Mary had to break up one ten-rod to put twelve in each group. If the problem had been about forty-eight cookies with twelve in each box, it would not have been necessary to trade tens for ones. Consequently, that would have been a much easier problem, but it would not have challenged her knowledge of base-ten concepts to the same degree. As with the Multiplication problem, if there were fewer than ten cookies in each box, children would have had to trade all the tens for ones, which would have made the use of base-ten materials superfluous.

Partitive Division Similar patterns are found in children's solutions of Partitive Division problems:

> *There are 42 children in the second grade. If we divide up into 3 teams with the same number of children on each team, how many children will there be on each team?*

> Mary gets out 4 ten-rods and 2 blocks. She puts 3 of the ten-rods into 3 separate locations. She trades the remaining ten-rod for 10 blocks and deals the 12 blocks to the 3 ten-rods. Each pile now contains 1 ten-rod and 4 blocks. She counts the blocks and answers, "14."

Again Mary had to change one of the tens into ones so that the blocks could be distributed into three groups. If there had been thirty-nine children in each grade, trading would not have been necessary; and if there had been six teams, it would not have been productive to use base-ten materials at all.

Children's Invented Strategies

Children's invented multiplication/division strategies generally make use of their knowledge of multidigit addition. They tend to use either a strategy in which they operate on the tens and ones separately, similar to the Combine Tens and Ones strategy used for addition and subtraction, or they use a doubling strategy.

Multiplication In the following examples, Pat first multiplied the tens and then the ones, and Sam used a doubling strategy:

The school bought 6 boxes of markers. There are 24 markers in each box. How many markers are there all together?

Pat: 6 twos is 12, so 6 twenties is 120. 3 fours is 12, and 3 more fours is 24. So it's 120 and 24, 144.

Sam: 24 and 24 is 48, and 48 and 48, that's 80 and 16, 96. That's 4 twenty-fours, so I need 2 more. So it's 96 and 48. Let's see, if I put 4 from the 48 with the 96, that gives me 100 and 48 becomes 44. So it's 144.

Measurement and Partitive Division The following are examples of strategies used to solve Measurement and Partitive Division problems:

The class baked 84 cookies. We want to put them into boxes to sell at the school bake sale. If we put 12 cookies into each box, how many boxes can we fill?

Sam: 12 and 12 is 24. That's 2. 24 and 24 is 48. That's 4. 48 and 48 is . . . No, wait. That's too much. 48 and 24 is 60 and 12, 72. That's 6, and I need 1 more 12. That makes 7.

There are 42 children in the second grade. If we divide up into 3 teams with the same number of children on each team, how many children will there be on each team?

Pat: If I put 10 in each group. That's 30. So there are 12 more. Oh, 3 fours is 12, so I can put 4 more with each 10. That's 14 on each team.

Sam used a doubling strategy for the Measurement Division problem, and Pat used a Tens–Ones strategy for the Partitive Division problem. The doubling strategy lends itself to solving a Measurement Division problem, but is difficult to apply to a Partitive Division problem. Note that the doubling strategy used for the previous Multiplication problem involved doubling the number in each group. For a Measurement Division problem, the number in each group is given, so it can be doubled. For the Partitive Division problem, the number in each group is the unknown, so there is nothing to double, which is why children do not generally use doubling for Partitive Division problems.

On the other hand, the Tens–Ones strategy works quite well for Partitive Division problems but is difficult to apply to Measurement Division situations. In a Partitive Division problem, the number of groups is known. The number in each group can be built up by successively adding tens and ones to each group until the required number is used up. Using a Tens–Ones strategy for the Measurement Division problem would involve breaking the number in the group up into tens and ones, which would not be difficult, but deciding how to use that information to find the number of groups is a difficult problem.

THE DEVELOPMENT OF MULTIDIGIT STRATEGIES

Strategies for adding, subtracting, multiplying, and dividing multidigit numbers develop as natural extension of the procedures that children use to solve problems involving single-digit numbers. Initially, they model problems involving two-digit numbers using individual counters in exactly the same way that they model problems with smaller numbers. Although the problems involve numbers greater than ten, children do not initially think of them any differently than problems that involve numbers less than ten. Their solutions make no use of base-ten concepts. When base-ten materials are first made available, children who use them to solve word problems often count by ones. The base-ten blocks simply serve as a convenient collection of counters that do not get all mixed up.

Modeling with Base-Ten Materials

Children come to recognize that they do not have to count all the blocks in the ten-rod each time they construct a set. At first many children are relatively inflexible in constructing and counting sets using tens. They may solve an addition problem by making each of the addends by counting collections of ten but then find the sum by counting the total by ones. Even after children progress to counting both addends and sums using tens, their conceptions are rather tenuous. For example, to solve a problem that involves finding the sum 37 + 28, a child may put out three ten-rods and seven cubes and two ten-rods and eight cubes. Next, the child counts the tens (10, 20, 30, 40, 50) and continues counting the ones (51, 52, 53, . . . 64, 65). The child's knowledge is sufficient to solve this problem using some concepts of base-ten numbers, but the child might not recognize that sixty-five can be represented as six tens and five ones as well as five tens and fifteen ones. The child simply generates an answer by counting by tens and then counting on by ones. The child is not confronted with the necessity of having to work out the relationship between alternative representations.

This same child might have more difficulty solving problems in which tens have to be exchanged for ones. For example, in attempting to solve a subtraction problem that involves taking thirty-eight from fifty-two, a child might not recognize that fifty-two can be represented as four tens and twelve ones in order to remove the three tens and eight ones. For the same reason, the child might also have difficulty with a Partitive Division problem in which forty-two objects are to be divided into three groups.

Over time, children come to use base-ten materials flexibly and efficiently. They recognize that a given number can be represented by a variety of different combinations of tens and ones and readily trade tens for ones and ones for tens to solve problems. As children's use of base-ten materials becomes more automatic, they come to depend less on manipulations of the physical materials themselves. This sets the stage for their construction of invented algorithms.

Invented Algorithms

Initially, children use mental procedures for situations in which it is relatively easy to keep track of the tens and ones. We present sequences of problems for which it is increasingly difficult for children to use invented algorithms in Figures 6.6 and 6.7.

FIGURE 6.6
Development of Invented Addition Strategies

Problem Stem _____ birds were sitting in a tree. _____ more birds joined them. How many birds were in the tree then?	
Numbers	*Some Possible Strategies*
60 + 20	"60, 70, 80" or "6 and 2 is 8, so 80."
65 + 20	"65, 75, 85" or "60 and 20 is 80. 5 more is 85."
65 + 8	"65 and 5 is 70. 3 more is 73."
65 + 24	"60 and 20 is 80. 5 and 4 is 9. So 89."
65 + 28	"60 and 20 is 80. 5 more is 85, and 8 more is 90 and 3. 93." or "60 and 20 is 80. 5 and 8 is 13, so 93."

FIGURE 6.7
Development of Invented Subtraction Strategies

Problem Stem _____ ducks were sitting in a pond. _____ flew away. How many ducks were left in the pond?	
Numbers	*Some Possible Strategies*
80 – 20	"80 take away 20 is 60" or "8 take away 2 is 6. So 60."
85 – 20	"80 take away 20 is 60. So 65."
85 – 7	"85 take away 5 is 80, and 2 more makes 78."
89 – 25	"80 take away 20 is 60. 9 take away 5 is 4. So 64."
83 – 25	"80 take away 20 is 60. Take away 5 is 55. Put back the 3 from the 83. That's 58."

Problems involving multiples of ten (60 + 20) are the easiest. Once a child understands that tens can be combined, it is not a great deal more complicated to add or subtract multiples of ten than it is to add or subtract one-digit numbers.

Monday, Anna played Nintendo for 20 minutes before school and for 60 minutes in the evening. How many minutes did she play Nintendo on Monday?

Julio: It's 80. It's like 2 and 6, only it's 2 tens and 6 tens, so that's 80.

Tanya: Mmm, 60 [pause], 70, 80. That's 80.

Problems in which one number is a multiple of ten (65 + 20) are slightly more difficult than problems in which both numbers are multiples of ten, and problems that do not involve regrouping (65 + 24) are quite a bit easier than problems that do (65 + 28). For problems involving multiples of ten or one multiple of ten, it often is not possible to distinguish between an Incrementing strategy and a Combining Tens and Ones strategy because there are no ones to combine separately. Problems in which a one-digit number is added to or subtracted from a two-digit number tend to encourage an Incrementing strategy, and problems that do not involve regrouping tend to encourage a Combining Tens and Ones strategy.

A caution is in order in using these problems. Children should not be expected to master one type of problem before they are given more difficult problems. That can lead to misconceptions and errors. For example, when children only study computation exercises that do not involve regrouping for an extended period of time, they frequently form the misconception that numbers are simply added within columns. That can lead to the following error:

$$
\begin{array}{r}
36 \\
+\ 47 \\
\hline
713
\end{array}
$$

Children generally have less difficulty inventing algorithms for addition than they do for subtraction, multiplication, or division; and, for most children, invented algorithms for subtraction, multiplication, and division appear to emerge considerably later than invented algorithms for addition.

Transitions

The transition to using more sophisticated strategies may be facilitated by teacher probes ("Is there an easier way to count those? Is there something you can do so that you can take away eight?"), by the selection of problem types and numbers in problems, and by having children listen to other children describe how they solved a given problem.

Development of multidigit concepts takes time. Children need time to explore the use of different representations and ways to think about numbers. Children need time to invent algorithms for solving problems. Even though some strategies may be inefficient, children cannot be rushed to use more efficient procedures without the potential loss of understanding.

LEARNING TO SOLVE PROBLEMS WITH MULTIDIGIT NUMBERS

Procedures for operating on two- and three-digit numbers develop as natural extensions of the strategies that children use to solve problems involving smaller numbers. Typically, base-ten materials such as ten-rods, or stacking cubes stored in rods of ten (Unifix cubes), are made available in kindergarten and each subsequent grade. Children initially use these materials as single units to solve problems by counting each of the individual units. The ten-rods simply serve as convenient collections of counters that do not get mixed up. With encouragement and the solving of many problems, children come to recognize that they do not have to count all the individual units in the ten-rods each time they construct a set. At first they may Count On By Ones from ten. Soon they construct two-digit quantities by making collections of tens and ones.

Children can be encouraged to use more advanced strategies by solving problems where use of tens is encouraged. As they do this over time, children become increasingly flexible and efficient in the use of base-ten materials. As they solve many problems, they come to depend less on the manipulations of physical materials and are able to abstract their solutions by inventing algorithms to add and subtract multidigit numbers without physical materials.

Consider how one first-grade teacher, starting on the first day of the school year, provided experiences that would lead to an understanding of base-ten concepts:

> On the first day of the school year, Ms. Gehn asked the children to solve a variety of problems involving numbers in the tens or twenties. Various materials were available including counters, number lines, and fingers. As is typical in CGI classrooms, Ms. Gehn did not show her students how to solve the problems, but asked them to solve the problems in any way they wished. After solving the problems, children reported their solution strategies to their classmates. During the rest of the week, children solved a variety of addition, subtraction, multiplication, and division word problems and shared their solution strategies. Most children directly modeled the problems with counters or used the number line.
>
> At the beginning of the second week, Ms. Gehn gave 10 ten-rods to each child and asked them to count the little cubes (units)

that could be seen in the bars. After everyone agreed that each ten-rod was made up of ten cubes, she asked how many little cubes there were in all 10 ten-rods. About half of the children counted the little cubes by ones and the others counted by tens. Children shared both strategies with the class, and a discussion ensued about which way was easier. To this point, Ms. Gehn provided the children with tools that would help them solve the problems using base-ten principles and gave them two-digit problems to solve. The teacher did not demonstrate how base-ten ideas would aid in problem solution. Although she drew the children's attention to the fact that there were ten units in each ten-rod, she placed little emphasis on base-ten number concepts. Some children attempted to use base-ten ideas to solve problems, but all children's knowledge of these ideas appeared limited.

Through the year, Ms. Gehn continued to ask children to solve problems where base-ten ideas would be useful, asked them to report their solutions, and drew the children's attention to solutions that involved base-ten ideas. She often asked children to solve problems in at least two ways and would emphasize that combining tens or counting by tens was easier than counting by ones.

7 | BEGINNING TO USE COGNITIVELY GUIDED INSTRUCTION

I first learned about CGI many moons ago. But it took awhile. It wasn't an easy task because you're learning about all the different types of strategies that children can use. You're also learning about all the different types of problems that there are. And so you're trying to put that all together. And then you're trying to make it usable for you. And I remember feeling very overwhelmed, going, "Wait a minute, what is that child doing?" I remember feeling at times very frustrated, saying, "Okay, I've got to look at this problem, now I've got to look at this type of strategy." And it wasn't an easy task. I had to go over it a lot. And then after a while it just becomes a part of you like everything else does. After you use it and you have it, it becomes easier. And it feels right. It's more comfortable.

Terese Kolan, second-grade teacher

My own personal experience with CGI is what I think of as a journey. When you are on this journey, there are going to be things as a teacher that you don't know. You learn from the CGI readings, you learn from the children. You don't learn it in a week. You don't go to one workshop and learn it. You don't even learn it in a couple of years. You continually improve.

Mazie Jenkins, first-grade teacher

The teachers quoted above provide clear evidence that becoming a CGI teacher takes time and doesn't happen by attending a few workshops. Because CGI is a radically new way to teach mathematics, many teachers feel uneasy as they begin to work with children to establish a CGI classroom. But almost all teachers have found that, although they felt uneasy as they started CGI, the rewards were worth the struggle for them and their students.

I saw children in my classroom who not only were able to do it, but they understood what they were doing. Kids were seeing themselves as problem solvers, and doing phenomenal things.

Mary Jo Yttri, kindergarten teacher

So for me, this year has been great! CGI has kind of validated what I have always innately felt but never really had the research background to do.

Kerri Burkey, second-grade teacher

We have found that one way to alleviate the uneasiness and to begin the "journey" that Ms. Jenkins describes is just to start. This chapter provides general information about starting your journey.

GETTING STARTED

Many teachers begin their CGI instruction by asking children to solve problems like those discussed in Chapters 2–6. Initially, a teacher might ask children to solve some simple problems set in contexts with which they are familiar. The teacher provides a variety of tools such as paper and pencil or counters, and encourages children to select the tool they wish to use. As children solve the problem, the teacher moves around and talks to various children about what they are doing, both to understand what they are doing and to provide support when necessary.

Consider one day in Almeta Hawkins's second-grade class. She started with the entire class clustered around her on the floor. After giving each child a copy of the problem to be solved, she had the children read the problem orally with her to ensure they understood it. Children were asked to go to a comfortable spot where there were tools available (paper, pencil, and cubes), and Ms. Hawkins moved from child to child asking him or her about solution strategies. Although the problem did not appear to be simple for the children, it is obvious that the children had engaged in similar tasks before because they were comfortable working the problem. Ms. Hawkins questioned them intensively about their solutions, apparently for several reasons: so that she could understand what they were doing, so that mistakes were discovered by the children, and so that the children would reflect on their own solution strategies. Most of her interactions with a child were directly related to the child's solution of the problem.

During the problem solving time, Ms. Hawkins selected three children who had solved the problem differently. During the strategy sharing time, these children shared their solutions with the class. She again questioned each child and involved the rest of the class in thinking about the strategies.

Although Ms. Hawkins typically uses whole class instruction for mathematics, she also has children work in small groups part of the time. Children are sometimes allowed to choose a group, or Ms. Hawkins might group children based on similarities in strategies used or problem types they can solve. Children do not stay in the same group for an extensive period of time.

Children in Ms. Hawkins's class are encouraged to keep mathematics journals in which they write their own problems and problems posed by the teacher. She records children's strategies and types of problems so that she can report specific information about children to their parents. Although Ms. Hawkins's skill and knowledge is clearly illustrated as she deals with her second-graders, her pattern of instruction is one that has been used by many beginning CGI teachers.

ORGANIZING A CLASS FOR CGI INSTRUCTION

Some teachers prefer starting their CGI work with a small group of children. In other classes, the entire class works on the same problem. Children who work more quickly than others are often asked to find two or even three ways to solve the problems. Sometimes teachers adapt the number sizes in a problem for certain children, or teachers provide different problems for different children. There is no optimal way to organize a CGI class. Whatever organization enables a teacher to get the children to solve problems and to listen to the students' problem-solving strategies is the optimal organization for that teacher.

Selecting Problems

Teachers select problem types and number sizes for many reasons. Sometimes teachers want a child to experience a certain type of problem with which she or he is having trouble. Take Annie Keith's classroom for example. When we observed her, she was working with a small group of children who had a wide range of problem-solving skills and who solved two Join (Change Unknown) problems as we watched.

It was quite obvious that two of the children were having trouble with the first problem:

Sunny had 7 pennies. His dad gave him some more, and now he has 11 pennies. How many did his dad give him?

After working with the children, Ms. Keith gave another problem of the same type:

Ashley has 9 toy rockets. How many more rockets does she need so that she will have 17 rockets all together?

A first reaction might be to question Ms. Keith's decision to use larger numbers when two children could not solve the same type of problem with smaller numbers. However, the second problem is worded so that it is easier for children to understand, and all four of the children were able to solve it successfully and explain their strategies. The two children who had difficulty with the first problem used a Direct Modeling strategy, one other child also used a Direct Modeling strategy, and the fourth child used a Counting strategy.

As we talked with Ms. Keith after the lesson, she revealed that she had deliberately chosen both of those problems with extreme care for those two children. She discussed how she chooses number sizes so that a child is challenged, yet has the possibility of success. For example, she said that Evelyn could use larger numbers for Result Unknown problems, but couldn't solve Join (Change Unknown) problems, so in this instance, Ms. Keith had chosen smaller numbers for the first problem. Ms. Keith recognized that the wording of the first problem was difficult for children and discussed how this had influenced the children's ability to solve that problem. She also reported that she uses multiplication and division problems quite early because these problems can be solved by direct modeling.

Sometimes teachers select problems to give children rich experiences in solving a variety of problems. At other times, teachers want children to improve their reporting skills, so they select relatively simple problems. Sometimes they select problems to encourage children to move to more mature strategies. Teachers choose contexts of problems that will be interesting, engaging, and understandable for children. The contexts are often related to something else the children are doing currently, such as a book they are reading, a social studies unit they are pursuing, or a field trip they are going to take.

Reporting Strategies

Problem solving is usually followed by sharing solution strategies. After the teacher has selected a problem, posed it to children, and waited a suitable period of time, she or he asks the children individually to report how they solved the problem to the class or a small group. When one child has reported a solution strategy, the teacher asks another child to report how he or she solved the problem. The teacher may ask how the two solutions are alike or different and if anyone solved it a different way. After several children have reported their solution strategies and the rest of the group has discussed them, the teacher reads another problem, often of a different type than the first, and the entire process is repeated. In many cases, students solve only two to four problems during one class period.

Teachers find that some general questions are quite useful for getting their students to talk about their thinking. "How did you solve that problem?", "Tell me how you got the answer?", "Can you tell me what you were thinking?" are questions teachers often use. Teachers may continue by asking probing questions based on what the child says or does. "Can you tell me why you separated those blocks?", "Why did you start with that number when you counted?", or "Can you tell me how you counted?" are probes that can provide more information for teachers as well as help the child to learn that the teacher wants a complete description of how the problem was solved.

Learning About Your Students

You have to have an understanding of where the children are, what kinds of number they can work with, and then proceed onward.

Terese Kolan, second-grade teacher

By understanding how the child is thinking, I'm able to see where they are, what level they're at, and what kinds of things I want to give them to move on to.

Michelle Garden, second-grade teacher

Before teachers begin to teach CGI, learning about what each child in the room knows appears difficult. In reality, most teachers have found that although they continue to learn about children's thinking over a long period of time, it is not difficult to acquire sufficient knowledge to begin using CGI. All it requires is having a beginning knowledge of the framework of children's thinking (Chapters 1–6), asking children to solve problems, having children report their thinking, and attending carefully to what the children report.

It means you have the information to look at the kids and understand where they are thinking about math. That enables you to look at the children and understand more about how they are thinking. It just helps you understand a whole lot more about where they are in their development.

Jennifer Beard, first-grade teacher

In order to gain initial understanding of the thinking of their children, some teachers formally interview each of their students at the beginning of the school year. Using the Children's Solution Strategies chart (Figure 3.7) as a guide, a teacher asks individual children to solve a variety of problems. The teacher continues to question each child until he or she understands the child's solution.

The first time that I was in my own classroom using this philosophy, I interviewed all my students. And for the first time I could really say what my kids really knew about problems. And what levels they were at. By the end of that first interview, I had so much knowledge about students.

Mazie Jenkins, first-grade teacher

Teachers also learn about their children as they observe, listen to, and question children during the ongoing instructional process. Consider one teacher's description of how she found out about her students' knowledge:

I observe them as I'm giving problems and walking around and seeing who is doing what and asking them what they are doing.

When they come up to me as I check their work, I can see what they have done. I might say to them: "Show me how you did this," or "Tell me what you're thinking about." I see kids looking at the clock, or I see kids looking at the number line, or I see kids with fingers or kids using manipulatives, or I see the strategies they are using.

> Susan Gehn, first- and third-grade teacher

Children's knowledge continually changes, particularly as they participate in many problem-solving experiences. Thus, knowledge about students must be continually updated, and this can done by observing and listening to children during class time, as the following report of what a teacher observed about one of her students shows:

The problem he was working on was the Separate (Result Unknown), and his first way of doing it was with the base-ten blocks. He had his answer. He was very confident in it. His answer was twenty-eight, and he knew how he got it, and that was fine. What I saw on his paper then was that he was beginning to write that problem in numbers. And I've never seen Michael write a problem out in an Invented Algorithm like he was doing today. It was the first time that he's attempted that.

> Kathy Statz, third-grade teacher

Seeing Change

One of the first things that teachers notice is that their students can solve more difficult problems than they anticipated. Children are remarkably inventive as they create their own problem-solving strategies.

I was really surprised what kids can do without any help from me at all. . . . And even now when some of the kids tell you how they solve a problem, you have to admire that, because in your wildest dreams you wouldn't have thought about doing it that way.

> Jennifer Beard, first-grade teacher

Let's look at some kindergarten children in Craig Meyer's class who were solving multiplication problems. Mr. Meyer was working with a small group of his students to whom he had read a Multiplication problem.

Mr. Meyer found 3 bird nests. Each nest had 5 eggs in it. How many eggs is that?

The children solved the problem, and each reported his or her solution strategy. Although there were various materials available, all of the children chose to solve the problem with paper and pencil or in their heads. Three children drew three circles (nests) with eggs inside them and found the total number of eggs in a variety of ways. By questioning each child, Mr. Meyer found out that some children had directly modeled the problem, others had counted, and one child said he just knew that three groups of five was fifteen. Mr. Meyer listened and questioned until he understood each strategy before he moved on to another Multiplication problem. As the children solved the new problem, some used counters, others used their fingers or a number line, and still others mentally counted by the number in each group. Children reported their solution strategies and Mr. Meyer questioned the children until he understood the strategy each child used.

Although these children were Mr. Meyer's most advanced students, their ability to solve mathematics problems was not particularly unusual for kindergarten children in CGI classes. Mr. Meyer's students solved two Multiplication problems that involved numbers up to thirty: three groups of five, and five groups of six. These children indicated clearly that they understood these problems, could solve them, and enjoyed working at this level.

Using Tools and Manipulative Materials

There are materials available for children to use as tools in CGI classes. Teachers make available simple counters, paper, pencils, and materials that can represent base-ten concepts (such as base-ten blocks or locking cubes such as linking cubes). These materials, however, are used differently than before. Traditionally, manipulative materials have been used to demonstrate mathematical ideas in non-CGI classrooms. In CGI classrooms instead of using materials to demonstrate the mathematical idea to be learned, all materials including fingers, counters, paper, and pencils are tools that a child can

FIGURE 7.1
Using Tools for Problem Solving

select to solve a particular problem. Teachers use the word "tool" to reflect exactly how they want children to think about materials, that is, as something that helps in performing a task, which in this case is solving mathematical problems. Almost any material can be used as a tool—providing that children understand its use and that the tool enables them to solve problems.

Almost all children come to kindergarten classes with an understanding of one of the most useful tools, namely, fingers. Fingers are readily available, they are familiar, they can be used to represent real-life objects, and almost all children use them even when teachers do not observe much overt use. Basically, children use fingers as counters and to keep track of things.

When numbers are larger than ten, it gets increasingly difficult to use fingers, so other materials that can serve as counters should be available as long as children choose to use them. Often children will solve many problems with more sophisticated strategies most of the time, but will return to the use of counters to directly model (or partially model) a problem that appears difficult to them.

> They know the counters are there. They can use them if they want to. [Though] once they have the confidence, they will usually take the risk of doing it without counters.
>
> Susan Gehn, first- and third-grade teacher

Counters sufficient to solve two-digit problems should be readily available to each child. They should be easy to use and store (perhaps in groups of ten to begin to develop base-ten knowledge), but they do not have to be elaborate or expensive. In fact, the elaborateness of some counters can prove a distraction from their main use, that is, to solve problems. It is easy for children to use the same set of counters (disks, cubes, etc.) to represent a variety of things that would be included in story problems. As children mature, they often make tallies or marks on paper, which also serve as counters.

In addition to counters, children need some tools that can be used to represent groups of ten. Some teachers use linking cubes, separate counters that can be joined together in groups of ten. Other teachers use base-ten blocks and units, which consist of individual cubes and solid bars ten units long, with each unit marked. Teachers and children use these materials in a variety of ways.

Although tools are of use to children in solving problems, they are also of major use to teachers as they try to understand what a child is thinking. As a teacher watches and/or listens to a child explain a solution, what the child is doing with the tool increases the teacher's knowledge of what is going on in the child's head.

BEGINNING THE JOURNEY

In order to get started teaching CGI, you need to be able to recognize and construct a variety of addition, subtraction, multiplication, and division word problems. You also need a beginning understanding of some common solution strategies used by many children. Then you can ask students to solve one problem in any way that they wish, with little help. As the children solve the problem, you can observe and ask questions about the solutions, and can then encourage the children to report to the rest of the class how they have solved the problem. If all the children solve the problem in the same way, you can ask them to solve it in a different way. Just by following these simple steps, you can initiate the journey towards becoming a CGI teacher.

8 | CGI CLASSROOMS

When you said, "You're sort of on your own, we will help you out, but you have free reign," it was clear that we were to make our own decisions, and I found that scary. But then after a while, I thought, they are really treating us like professionals, like we know something, instead of spoon-feeding us.

Ann Badeau, second-grade teacher

Teaching is complex. Almost every minute, a teacher makes a decision about what to teach, how to teach, who to call on, how fast the lesson should move, how to respond to a child, and so on. Although decisions are dependent on many things (the principal, the parents, the textbook, etc.), because of the intimate knowledge of students that teachers have, no one else can make these immediate decisions about what to do in the classroom.

Because immediate teaching decisions cannot be made by anyone but the teacher, we do not attempt to provide explicit directions for how to organize a classroom or how to implement instruction. However, we can provide some information about what experienced CGI teachers have done and describe major similarities of classrooms developed by CGI teachers.

SIMILARITIES OF CGI CLASSROOMS

It is not simple to describe a typical CGI classroom because each one is unique and can appear to be quite different from other CGI classrooms. In some classes, whole group instruction is used. In other classes, children spend most of their time working in learning centers. In some classes, children create many of the problems to be solved, whereas in others the teacher chooses the problems. In spite of the apparent diversity, there are similarities that can be seen across most CGI classrooms. Consider the following episode from Mary Jo Yttri's kindergarten class.

Ms. Yttri was working with her entire kindergarten class sitting in a circle on the rug. She read a Join (Result Unknown) problem aloud:

6 tiger sharks were swimming around together. 5 more tiger sharks joined them. How many tiger sharks were there all together?

First, the children solved the problem individually using materials they had chosen. When they had finished, Ms. Yttri asked four individuals to report their problem solutions. Although all four children reported Joining All strategies, each had used a different material. One child had used pegs, another dominoes, another tally marks on a slate, and another had combined a Derived Fact strategy with the Joining All strategy. Ms. Yttri listened carefully and asked questions to clarify the child's response if necessary. She expected the other children to listen also. After four children had finished reporting, Ms. Yttri posed another problem, and the process was repeated.

Note that the teacher posed a problem and let the children choose how they would solve it. Children were asked to report their solutions while the teacher and the other children listened. The teacher questioned each child until the solution strategy was clear. This sequence is very typical of CGI classrooms. Teachers pose a problem which they or the children have written, children are given time to solve the problem while the teachers move around the classroom and ask questions, and children report how they solved the problem. This sequence is then repeated.

In many CGI classes, after children have reported their solutions, the teachers ask the children to compare the various strategies that have been reported. For example, Ms. Yttri might ask the children in her class how each of the strategies used to solve the shark problem were alike. Through careful questioning, the teacher could elicit evidence that most children had modeled each of the sets and then counted to find the answer, even though they used different materials to model the sharks.

Basing the Curriculum on Problem Solving

The neat thing about problem solving is you can take one problem, and you can go through an entire list of topics that you think are important in your math curriculum, and with one problem you can really address almost every topic that you feel is important.

Susan Gehn, first- and third-grade teacher

In CGI classes, all learning activities require problem solving. Children learn concepts and computational skills as they solve a variety of mathematics problems often set in story contexts like those discussed earlier. Sometimes problems are set in other formats like writing number sentences that equal a certain number, finding several ways to add two- or three-digit numbers, or discussing a mathematical concept such as odd or even numbers. The critical consideration is that each child is actively involved in deciding how best to resolve a mathematical situation. It is when children decide upon a strategy to represent a mathematical situation and implement that strategy that problem solving takes place. Consider these problem-solving situations that occured in Mazie Jenkins's first-grade classroom.

One group used counters to find ways to make ten, wrote the number sentence to match what they had done, and then told a story (a word problem) to go with the number sentence. Another group worked with the teacher to make the number thirty (the day's date; e.g., 5 + 5 + 5 + 5 + 5 + 5), solved word problems (written by the teacher) which involved the number 30, and then wrote story problems about thirty.

In this class, there were at least three kinds of problem solving: writing a word problem to go with a story, combining numbers in a variety of ways to make thirty, and solving story problems written by the teacher. As the children engaged in problem solving, they were practicing skills and learning concepts at the same time that they were solving problems.

Unlike traditional instruction in which the content to be learned is clearly sequenced (addition before subtraction, etc.) and where children learn skills before they use them to solve problems, the curriculum in CGI classes is integrated. For example, children do not learn number facts as isolated bits of information. Rather they learn them as they repeatedly solve problems, so that they begin to see relationships between the various facts. In the following quote, a second-grade teacher describes the way she handled the learning of basic facts before she learned about CGI and how her approach has changed:

> I wasn't very happy with the way things were in math. We used to have to give these timed tests, and I'd have kids that would cry, and I would have parents that would complain, and I would have kids with tummyaches on the day of the test. I felt like we were always beating our head against the wall. And I always thought, why are we doing this? What purpose is this serving in the end? . . . Now things are different. I don't do the timed tests. My children learn their facts from solving problems, and they know them as well as they ever did.
> Ann Badeau, second-grade teacher

In summary, children in CGI classes learn mathematics with understanding through problem solving. Both word problems and symbolic problems are the vehicles through which children learn mathematical concepts and skills. Although teachers choose problems so that they will enhance children's development, in most cases, teachers do not provide explicit instruction on problem-solving strategies. Instead children develop their own problem-solving strategies, which become more efficient and abstract over time. Skills and number facts are learned in the process of problem solving and are thus learned with understanding rather than learned as isolated pieces of information.

When the kids listen to each other, they understand it better than when they hear it directly from me. It makes more sense to them . . . I really see a lot of learning going on by children listening to the other children, I really do. I mean I see some of the slower kids really picking up on concepts . . . really learning a lot from listening to the other kids.

Susan Gehn, first- and third-grade teacher

Closely integrated with problem solving is communicating about one's thinking. This communication usually takes the form of talking, writing, or drawing pictures about how problems have been solved, and it serves a variety of purposes. It encourages children to think about or reflect on what they have done. It encourages understanding, because in order to be able to report (which becomes very important to children), they have to understand what they have done. It also enables the teacher to assess a child's thinking while at the same time allowing other children to hear a variety of strategies.

There are many ways that children communicate their thinking in CGI classrooms. Reporting can be done orally or with paper and pencil; it can take place in large or small groups or during individual interactions with the teacher or another child. Children may demonstrate their strategies with the materials that they have used to solve the problem, or they can just describe what they did. For example, a child who used base-ten blocks to directly model a Join (Result Unknown) problem with thirty-eight and twenty-five described how she solved the problem this way:

Well, I made the 38; that was 3 tens and 8 ones. Then I made the 25; that was 2 tens and 5 ones. I had to find out how much that was. First I counted the tens and I got 50. Then I kept going from there and counted all the little blocks that were left. There were 63 all together.

Having students report on their thinking is beneficial to both the teacher and the children. It encourages children to reflect on their strategies and, thus, come to understand their strategies better. In CGI classes, children operate at many different levels because children have the latitude to use a strategy that makes sense to them at the time. There is no prevalent strategy that all children use at a particular point in time. The variety of strategies in use at any given time gives children the opportunity to learn more advanced strategies by listening to and interacting with other students who are using them. When a student was asked why she was using a particular strategy, she said, "Why, I listened to Patrice. And because I listened to her, I wanted to try it. And you know, it really does work."

This child was using a higher level strategy than she would have used if she had not listened to Patrice. Another child, a second-grader named Sarah, always counted by ones. She would sit there and count on until one day when she heard somebody else using a strategy that started with 38 and continued 48, 58, 68. Sarah asked that child, "How do you know?" And the child explained it to her. From that day on, Sarah used that same strategy. Children sharing strategies enables other children because they're listening carefully. If they are ready for it—and they have to be cognitively ready for that strategy—it might work for them.

Creating a Climate for Communication

Initially, reporting how a problem has been solved is not easy, but it becomes easier as children have many experiences reporting their strategies. Children are continually asked to report their thinking, and their peers are expected to listen to and value each other's thinking. Gradually, children come to recognize that their thinking is important, and they come to value the process of doing mathematics.

Closely related to the idea of valuing each child's thinking is the growing realization that there is no one best or "right" way to solve any problem. Any strategy that works and can be explained is important and correct. When a teacher expects and values a diversity of solution strategies, children realize that multiple strategies are not only acceptable but desirable. Thus, no one's solution strategy is any better than anyone else's, and each child's thinking becomes important to everyone.

Teaching for Understanding

Because understanding is synonymous with seeing relationships, emphasizing relationships helps to develop understanding. No one can give knowledge to

FIGURE 8.1
*Children Talking About
Their Strategies*

anyone else. Each individual must develop understanding by constructing relationships. This does not mean that a teacher can never tell children anything; sometimes the best way to construct a relationship is to have someone else point it out. However, even when children are told something, in order to understand they must be able to comprehend the relationship.

Think about how relationships can be emphasized. Children could be asked to solve the following problems:

> *Maria has 8 guppies, and Andy has 7 guppies. How many guppies do they have all together?*

> *Andy found 15 shells. He gave 8 to Maria and kept the rest. How many did he keep?*

Both problems involve the same numbers. As children work and solve similar problems like these, they begin to recognize the relationships between eight, seven, and fifteen.

Children in CGI classes learn their number facts as well as, if not better, than children in more traditional classes. And because they spend relatively little time on direct practice of the number facts, their increased knowledge comes from the many opportunities they have to develop understanding of the relationships between the number facts. Learning number facts is made much easier by understanding that facts are related in specific ways and that there are principles governing these relationships. The basic principle that children should be encouraged to observe as early as possible is that number facts are related and that these relationships can be used to simplify the process of solving problems. Thus, teachers ask questions designed to focus students' attention on these relationships.

Not only are there relationships between number facts, there are also relationships between solution strategies such as Direct Modeling, Counting, and using Grouping By Ten to solve problems. When children experience many solution strategies, they come to see how strategies are related. For example, first/second-grade teacher Annie Keith asked children to solve two Join (Change Unknown) with different numbers:

$$7 + \square = 11, 9 + \square = 17$$

After problem solving, she asked the children if they noticed any similarities in the solution strategies for the two problems.

Children mature in their use of strategies when they see the relationships between less mature and more mature strategies. And teachers play a vital role in helping children see these relationships. Consider what Kathy Statz did in her third-grade class to help all of her children see such relationships. Children in this class were expected to solve problems in two distinct ways and to be able to report to both the teacher and their peers what they had done. Seeing that two distinct solution strategies resulted in the same answers focused children's attention on the strategies' similarities. Take Michael for example. He first solved a Separate (Result Unknown) problem by Direct Modeling with base-ten blocks. Ms. Statz noticed that he had also written an Invented Algorithm on his paper but had made an error. She worked with him by asking him questions that focused his attention on the relationships between his Direct Modeling strategy and his Invented Algorithm strategy. Although it is a bit unclear whether he totally understood, he reported his strategy to the class later.

In her second-grade class, Terese Kolan emphasized a different kind of relationship, that of symbols and their solutions to problems. After her children solved a problem, she asked them to write number sentences to represent their solutions. A similar emphasis on developing an understanding of the relationship between Direct Modeling and symbols was evident in Kathy Statz's third-grade class.

THE ROLE OF THE TEACHER

I remember the first time you came into my classroom. I always crack up when I think about this. I was at the board telling the children how to carry their ones to the tens' and that kind of business. And now it's completely different than that. I mean, I don't tell the kids how to do it, and they figure out ways to add multi-digit numbers on their own. And so it's like a complete reversal, where I'm not the center focus of instruction like I used to be. Now they're the center; their thinking is the center, and that's what it should be. For years the opposite way is the way I—we all— taught. And the kids, they'd go and take these tests, and if they'd forget which step they were on, they wouldn't know how to do it. So they weren't really solving problems from what they thought. They solved problems from what you told them to do. And so that is a big change. . . . Each child has his or her own level of understanding, and I think if you base instruction on the child's understanding it is so much better.

Ann Badeau, second-grade teacher

A CGI teacher's role is active. CGI teachers continually upgrade their understanding of how each child thinks, select activities that will engage all the children in problem solving and enable their mathematical knowledge to grow, and create a learning environment where all children are able to communicate about their thinking and feel good about themselves in relation to mathematics.

The following example illustrates a second-grade teacher, Ann Badeau, using knowledge of children's thinking to actively encourage David to move toward more mature solution strategies. Ms. Badeau asked David, a second-grade child, to solve the following Join (Change Unknown) problem:

If you have 15 acorns, how many more would you have to pick up to have 46 acorns?

David counted on from 15 to 46, kept track of the counts, and said "31." When he reported the strategy, the teacher understood what he did, and accepted it, but decided that David could be encouraged to use a somewhat more sophisticated strategy based on tens:

Ms. Badeau: Okay. You know we have tried counting by tens in our room. Remember how we've counted like 10, 20, 30. I was wondering, could you ever count by tens starting at 15? How would you do that?
David: 25, 35, 45, 55, 65, 75, 85, 95.
Ms. Badeau: Okay, you can do that. I was wondering, just for an example. How would you figure this one [the same problem about acorns] out if you did that?
David: Well, I could go from 15 to 45 and add 1 more.
Ms. Badeau: But how would you do that? I'm just curious.
David: 15, 25, 45, wait, 15, 25, 35—
Ms. Badeau: Are you counting by tens?
David: These are the tens [points to three marks he had made on paper]. 45 and 1 more would be 46. [3 tens and 1 more is 31.]

It should be noted that although Ms. Badeau encouraged David to invent his own ways to solve problems, her role was quite active. She listened carefully and then used what she knew to lead him to use and develop his base-ten knowledge to solve the problem.

Understanding Students' Mathematical Thinking

I listen to kids more, for one thing . . . I am so much more aware of what the kids can really do that before I would never have thought about first grade trying multiplication and division. . . . Then when I gave the children the opportunity and saw how they really do . . . solve those problems, now I realize that they can do them and give them the opportunity to do it.

Susan Gehn, first- and third-grade teacher

The framework of children's thinking, discussed in Chapters 1–6, provides a basis for understanding critical components of almost all children's thinking. Although it appears complex at first, its coherence becomes more and more visible as a CGI classroom develops. Rather than having to remember unrelated details, each child's thinking can be understood in relation to the framework. The framework provides a basis for understanding why a child is able to solve certain problems and not able to solve others. The path of development of ideas becomes visible, so it is possible to predict how children's thinking will grow.

PLANNING FOR INSTRUCTION

In CGI classes, decisions about what to teach and when to teach it are based on what children understand. For example, in many kindergarten classes, children solve addition, subtraction, multiplication, and division problems that can be directly modeled. For very young children, solving simple Multiplication problems gives them experience with grouping as a prelude to development of the major base-ten idea of grouping by ten. As children mature, solving two- and three-digit problems enables them to develop number sense as well as to discover how to work with groups of ten. When children understand the concept of grouping in concrete situations, they can work more directly on base-ten concepts. (For more about children's understanding of the base-ten number system, see Chapter 6.) Instruction is thus based on what children understand and can learn.

Using Knowledge of Children's Thinking

Using knowledge of children's thinking is not easy, and experienced CGI teachers report to us that they continually grow in their abilities to use their children's knowledge to select problems, to question children in a way that both elicits their thinking and helps them in problem solving, and to understand their children's thinking. All of this information helps the teachers structure the mathematical learning environment so that the children develop their mathematical knowledge. In very general terms, CGI teachers understand the way children think, understand what makes problems easier or more difficult to solve, and then make decisions that enable children to engage in successful problem solving with problems that are neither too easy nor too difficult.

> I have to decide where the kids are, and then I have to use my knowledge about where they're at in my class, and then I have to come up with the story problems to get these kids to build on what they already know.
> Susan Gehn, first- and third-grade teacher

Problems that can be solved by children at certain levels of development are often clustered together. For example, all problems that can be easily solved with a Direct Modeling strategy can be given in the same time frame. Quite young children can solve addition/subtraction and multiplication/division problems that can be directly modeled, and it is not necessary for children to be able to easily solve addition/subtraction problems before they are asked to solve multiplication/division problems. Similarly, children can solve many types of problems by various counting strategies. Problems such as Start Unknown problems, which require more sophisticated understandings, can be postponed until the child's knowledge and abilities mature.

Encouraging Children's Mathematical Development

CGI teachers provide problem-solving experiences that enable each child's knowledge to grow. Ideas that are important for children to learn are not ignored, nor taught incidentally. Problem-solving experiences are chosen in which the ideas to be learned can be explored. Through sensitive questioning, children can be encouraged to focus on and discuss the selected ideas; thus, their mathematical knowledge grows and develops. Consider Karen Falkner's explanation of why she chose to ask her second-graders to solve the following problem:

> *Spider went to the garden. He dug 75 yams. If he put 10 yams in each bag, how many bags did he fill? How many yams were in the bag that wasn't full?*

> I gave the problem, which is basically talking about place value [base-ten] understanding about 75 because I was looking for the kids who could say, like Nick did, "Well, I know from where the 7 is. That's 7 tens, and that's 70. So that would be 7 bags." Or looking for the kids who wanted to directly model it, I was looking to see if I would get any kids who would actually model it like a division problem.

Children choose strategies to solve problems for a variety of reasons, and they can be encouraged to move to more mature solution strategies. Consciously selecting problems to be solved, asking children to solve problems in more than one way, being sure that children hear solution strategies that are different from the ones they used, and discussing how various solution strategies are alike or different are just a few ways that children can be encouraged to develop their problem-solving skills.

Almost all CGI teachers find that listening to and understanding their students' thinking is one of the most rewarding things that has happened to them professionally. These teachers become strong advocates of the importance of understanding children's thinking, and they use that understanding to select problems that challenge children to engage in problem solving and that children are willing to work at to solve.

APPENDIX
The Research Base for Cognitively Guided Instruction

Cognitively Guided Instruction is based on an integrated program of research focused on the development of students' mathematical thinking; on instruction that influences that development; on teachers' knowledge and beliefs that influence their instructional practices; and on the way that teachers' knowledge, beliefs, and practices are influenced by their understanding of students' mathematical thinking. Our research has been cyclic. We started with explicit knowledge about the development of children's mathematical thinking (Carpenter 1985), which we used as a context to study teachers' knowledge of students' mathematical thinking (Carpenter et al. 1988) and the way teachers might use knowledge of students' thinking in making instructional decisions (Carpenter et al. 1989). We found that although teachers had a great deal of intuitive knowledge about children's mathematical thinking, it was fragmented and, as a consequence, generally did not play an important role in most teachers' decision making (Carpenter et al. 1988). If teachers were to be expected to plan instruction based on their knowledge of students' thinking, they needed some coherent basis for making instructional decisions. To address this problem, we designed CGI to help teachers construct conceptual maps of the development of children's mathematical thinking in specific content domains (Carpenter, Fennema, and Franke 1996).

In a series of studies (Carpenter et al. 1989; Fennema et al. 1993; Fennema et al. 1996) we found that learning to understand the development of children's mathematical thinking could lead to fundamental changes in teachers' beliefs and practices and that these changes were reflected in students' learning. The studies provided sites for examining the development of children's mathematical thinking in situations in which their intuitive strategies for solving problems were a focus for reflection and discussion. Other studies (Carpenter et al. 1993; Carpenter et al. 1996) provided new perspectives on the development of children's mathematical thinking and on the instructional contexts that support that development, which in turn has led to revisions in our approach to teacher development.

In the sections that follow, we discuss the research base for CGI with respect to (a) children's thinking, (b) teachers' knowledge and beliefs about children's thinking and the relation of teachers' knowledge and beliefs to their students' achievement, (c) the effect of the CGI Professional Development Program on teachers' knowledge, beliefs, and practice, and (d) the achievement of students in CGI classes. Keep in mind that this division does not represent a sequence in which the research was conducted. In fact most of our studies have crossed several categories.

Research on Children's Thinking

The model of children's thinking that is the basis for CGI is built on an extensive research base. The research support for our analysis of the development of addition/subtraction concepts was synthesized in Carpenter 1985; Fuson 1992; Gutstein and Romberg 1996; and Verschaffel and De Corte 1993. The research support for our analysis of multiplication/division and the general notion of modeling was reported in Carpenter et al. 1993 and Greer 1992. The analysis of the development of multidigit concepts was supported by research reported in Carpenter et al. 1998; and Fuson et al. 1997.

A study that we conducted with kindergarten children (Carpenter et al. 1993) provided some results that workshop leaders have found to be a provocative context for discussion. In this study we found that, by the end of kindergarten, children in CGI classes could solve a variety of problems by modeling the action or relations described in the problems. Many teachers and curriculum developers considered the problems too difficult for young children, and the results provided compelling support that children as young as kindergarten can invent strategies to solve a variety of problems if they are given the opportunity to do so. Some of the results are summarized in Figure A.1. In almost every case, the children used the predicted Direct Modeling strategies, although a few did use Counting strategies for several problems.

Teachers' Knowledge and Beliefs About Children's Thinking

In a study of teachers who had not participated in the CGI Professional Development Program (PDP), we found that teachers had a great deal of intuitive knowledge about children's mathematical thinking; however because that knowledge was fragmented it generally did not play an important role in most teachers' decision making (Carpenter et al. 1988). This study indicated that teachers have informal knowledge of children's thinking that can be built upon in the CGI Professional Development Program (PDP). In particular, teachers can identify differences between problem types, and they have some idea of many of the modeling and counting strategies that children often use. But most teachers' understanding of problems and strategies is not well connected, and most do not appreciate the critical role that Modeling and Counting strategies play in children's thinking or understand that more than a few students are capable of using Derived Facts.

This study also showed that teachers' knowledge of their students' thinking was related to student achievement. Students of teachers who

Problem	Percent of Children Who Solved Each Problem Correctly
Carla has 7 dollars. How many more dollars does she have to earn so that she will have 11 dollars to buy a puppy?	74
James has 12 balloons. Amy has 7 balloons. How many more balloons does James have than Amy?	67
Tad had 15 guppies. He put 3 guppies in each jar. How many jars did Tad put guppies in?	71
19 children are going to the circus. 5 children can ride in each car. How many cars will be needed to get all 19 children to the circus?	64
Maria had 3 packages of cupcakes. There were 4 cupcakes in each package. She ate 5 cupcakes. How many are left?	64
19 children are taking a minibus to the zoo. The bus has 7 seats. How many children will have to sit 3 to a seat, and how many can sit 2 to a seat?	51

FIGURE A.1
Kindergarten Children's Success in Solving Various Word Problems

knew more about their students' thinking had higher levels of achievement in problem solving than students of teachers who had less knowledge of their students' thinking. In a related study with the same teachers (Peterson et al. 1989), we found that classes of teachers whose beliefs were more consistent with principles of CGI tended to have higher levels of achievement than classes of teachers whose beliefs were less consistent with principles of CGI.

The Effect of Participating in CGI Professional Development Programs on Teachers' Knowledge, Beliefs, and Instruction

In the first CGI study, which investigated the effect of the CGI PDP on teachers, we focused entirely on addition and subtraction with first-grade teachers (Carpenter et al. 1989). The study was an experimental study in which we compared twenty CGI teachers with twenty control teachers. We found that CGI teachers placed greater emphasis on problem solving and less on computational skills, expected more multiple-solution strategies rather than a single method, listened to their children more, and knew more about their children's thinking than did control teachers.

Whereas the initial experimental study compared different groups of teachers, a three-year longitudinal study of twenty-one teachers (Fennema et al. 1996) explicitly examined the nature and pattern of change among teachers and the relation between beliefs and instruction. Several levels of beliefs and practice in becoming a CGI teacher were identified. Level 1 teachers believe that children need to be explicitly taught how to do mathematics. Instruction in their classes is usually guided by an adopted text and focuses on the learning of specific skills. Teachers generally demonstrate the steps in a procedure as clearly as they can, and the children practice applying the procedures. Children are expected to solve problems using standard procedures, and there is little or no discussion of alternative solutions. Level 2 teachers begin to question whether children need explicit instruction in order to solve problems, and the teachers alternately provide opportunities for children to solve problems using their own strategies and show the children specific methods.

Level 3 is a turning point. Level 3 teachers believe that children can solve problems without having a strategy provided for them, and they act accordingly. They do not present procedures for children to imitate. Children spend most of mathematics class solving and reporting their solutions to a variety of problems. Classrooms are characterized by students talking about mathematics, both to other students and to the teacher. Children report a variety of strategies and compare and contrast different strategies. In sum, Level 3 teachers epitomize the characteristics that distinguished CGI teachers from control teachers in the initial experimental study. Their classrooms are strongly influenced by their understanding of children's thinking, they know appropriate problems to pose and questions to ask to elicit children's thinking, and they understand and appreciate the variety of solutions that children construct to solve them.

What distinguishes Level 3 teachers from Levels 4a and 4b teachers is their use of what they learn from listening to students to make instructional decisions. Whereas Level 3 teachers apply their understanding of children's thinking to select appropriate problems and accurately assess their own students' thinking by listening to the strategies they use, Level 4a and 4b teachers conceptualize instruction in terms of the thinking of the children in their classes. Furthermore, they have a more fluid perspective of their students' thinking; they not only apply their knowledge to assess their own students' thinking and to plan instruction, but they also regard it as a framework for developing a deeper understanding of children's thinking in general. In the terms of Richardson (1994), teachers regard their knowledge as a basis for engaging in "practical inquiry." For these teachers, our research-based analyses of children's thinking are not conceived as fixed models to learn but as a focus for reflection on children's mathematical thinking, which helps them organize their knowledge and interpret their students' thinking. These teachers continually reflect back on, modify, adapt, and expand their models in light of what they hear from their students.

By the end of the study, nineteen of the twenty-one teachers in the longitudinal study were at Level 3 or higher (seven were at Levels 4a and 4b). Eighteen of the twenty-one teachers had changed at least one level in beliefs and practice, and twelve had changed at least two levels.

Case studies (Fennema et al. 1992; Fennema et al. 1993; Franke et al. in press) supported these findings and provided rich descriptions of teacher change and of the ways teachers have implemented principles of CGI in their classrooms. These studies confirmed the finding of the longitudinal study that change is difficult and takes place over an extended period of time. Developing an understanding of children's thinking provides a basis for change, but change occurs as teachers attempt to apply their knowledge to understand their own students. It is a slow dialectic process, with changes in knowledge and instruction building upon one another. But almost all teachers in our studies have changed in fundamental ways.

The case studies not only showed how teachers can change by learning about children's thinking; they also demonstrated how much can be accomplished by both teachers and students when children's thinking becomes a primary focus for instruction. The studies illustrate how teachers provide an environment in which children's thinking is the focus, children communicate about mathematics, children construct their own procedures for solving problems, and concepts are developed through problem solving. The case studies described exceptional teachers engaged in the kind of teaching that captures the spirit of current reform recommendations and documented how much children are capable of learning in such environments.

Student Achievement

In the initial experimental study (Carpenter et al. 1989), we found that CGI classes had significantly higher levels of achievement in problem solving than control classes had. Although there was significantly less emphasis on number skills in CGI classes, there was no difference between the groups in achievement on a test of number skills. In fact, there was some evidence that CGI students actually had better recall of number facts than did students in the control classes. A standardized achievement test also was administered in this study, and no differences were found between CGI and control classes on this test.

In a related study using the same measures, Villasenor and Kepner (1993) found that urban students in CGI classes performed significantly higher than a matched sample of students in traditional classes. Further discussion of the effectiveness of CGI with students from typically underachieving groups can be found in Carey et al. 1995 and Peterson, Fennema, and Carpenter 1991.

The longitudinal study (Fennema et al. 1996) extended the findings of the initial experimental study. By the third year of the study, the concepts and problem-solving performance of the classes of every teacher were substantially higher than they had been at the beginning of the study. Overall performance in skills showed no change. Improved performance in concepts and problem solving appeared to be cumulative, with students having longer participation in CGI classes showing greater gains in the upper grades during the second and third years of the study. Changes in student achievement reflected changes in teacher practice. For each teacher in the study, substantial improvement in the performance in concepts and problem solving of the teacher's students followed directly a change in the level of the teacher's practice.

Thus, our studies consistently demonstrate that CGI students show significant gains in problem solving. These gains reflect the emphasis on problem solving in CGI classes. On the other hand, in spite of the decreased emphasis on drill and practice, there is no commensurate loss in skills.

REFERENCES

Carey, D. A., E. Fennema, T. P. Carpenter, and M. L. Franke. 1995. "Equity and Mathematics Education." In *New Directions in Equity for Mathematics Education*, edited by W. Secada, E. Fennema, and L. Byrd. New York: Teachers College Press.

Carpenter, T. P. 1985. "Learning to Add and Subtract: An Exercise in Problem Solving." In *Teaching and Learning Mathematical Problem Solving: Multiple Research Perspectives*, edited by E. A. Silver. Hillsdale, NJ: Erlbaum.

Carpenter, T. P., E. Ansell, M. L. Franke, E. Fennema, and L. Weisbeck. 1993. "Models of Problem Solving: A Study of Kindergarten Children's Problem-Solving Processes." *Journal for Research in Mathematics Education* 24 (5): 427–440.

Carpenter, T. P., E. Ansell, L. Levi, M. L. Franke, and E. Fennema. 1996. Building Multidigit Number Concepts on Children's Informal Mathematical Thinking: Case Studies of Two First-Grade Teachers. Manuscript submitted for publication.

Carpenter, T. P., E. Fennema, and M. L. Franke. 1996. "Cognitively Guided Instruction: A Knowledge Base for Reform in Primary Mathematics Instruction." *The Elementary School Journal* 97 (1): 3–20.

Carpenter, T. P., E. Fennema, P. L. Peterson, and D. A. Carey. 1988. "Teachers' Pedagogical Content Knowledge of Students' Problem Solving in Elementary Arithmetic." *Journal for Research in Mathematics Education* 19: 385–401.

Carpenter, T. P., E. Fennema, P. L. Peterson, C. P. Chiang, and M. Loef. 1989. "Using Knowledge of Children's Mathematics Thinking in Classroom Teaching: An Experimental Study." *American Educational Research Journal* 26 (4): 499–531.

Carpenter, T. P., M. L. Franke, V. Jacobs, and E. Fennema. 1998. "A Longitudinal Study of Invention and Understanding in Children's Multidigit Addition and Subtraction." *Journal for Research in Mathematics Education* 29: 3–20.

Fennema, E., T. P. Carpenter, M. L. Franke, and D. A. Carey. 1992. "Learning to Use Children's Mathematics Thinking: A Case Study." In *Schools, Mathematics, and the World of Reality*, edited by R. Davis and C. Maher. Needham Heights, MA: Allyn and Bacon.

Fennema, E., T. P. Carpenter, M. L. Franke, L. Levi, V. Jacobs, and S. Empson. 1996. "Learning to Use Children's Thinking in Mathematics Instruction: A Longitudinal Study." *Journal for Research in Mathematics Education* 27 (4): 403–434.

Fennema, E., M. L. Franke, T. P. Carpenter, and D. A. Carey. 1993. "Using Children's Knowledge in Instruction." *American Educational Research Journal* 30 (3): 555–583.

Franke, M. L., E. Fennema, T. C. Carpenter, E. Ansell, and J. Behrend. In press. "Understanding Teachers' Self-Sustaining Change in the Context of Mathematics Instruction: The Role of Practical Inquiry." *Teaching and Teacher Education*.

Fuson, K. C. 1992. "Research on Whole Number Addition and Subtraction." In *Handbook of Research on Mathematics Teaching and Learning*, edited by D. Grouws. New York: Macmillan.

Fuson, K. C., D. Wearne, J. C. Hiebert, H. G. Murray, P. G. Human, A. I. Olivier, T. P. Carpenter, and E. Fennema. 1997. "Children's Conceptual Structures for Multidigit Numbers and Methods of Multidigit Addition and Subtraction." *Journal of Research in Mathematics Education* 28: 130–162.

Greer, B. 1992. "Multiplication and Division as Models of Situations." In *Handbook of Research on Mathematics Teaching and Learning*, edited by D. Grouws. New York: Macmillan.

Gutstein, E., and T. A. Romberg. 1996. "Teaching Children to Add and Subtract." *The Journal of Mathematical Behavior* 14: 283–324.

Hiebert, J., T. P. Carpenter, E. Fennema, K. Fuson, P. Human, H. Murray, A. Olivier, and D. Wearne. 1997. *Making Sense: Teaching and Learning Mathematics with Understanding*. Portsmouth, NH: Heinemann.

Peterson, P. L., E. Fennema, and T. P. Carpenter. 1991. "Using Children's Mathematical Knowledge." In *Teaching Advanced Skills to Educationally Disadvantaged Students*, edited by B. Means. Menlo Park, CA: SRI International.

Peterson, P. L., E. Fennema, T. P. Carpenter, and M. Loef. 1989. "Teachers' Pedagogical Content Beliefs in Mathematics." *Cognition and Instruction* 6 (1): 1–40.

Richardson, V. 1994. "Conducting Research on Practice." *Educational Researcher* 23 (5): 5–10.

Verschaffel, L., and E. De Corte. 1993. "A Decade of Research on Word-Problem Solving in Leuven: Theoretical, Methodological, and Practical Outcomes." *Educational Psychology Review* 5 (3): 1–18.

Villasenor, A., and H. S. Kepner. 1993. "Arithmetic from a Problem-Solving Perspective: An Urban Implementation." *Journal for Research in Mathematics Education* 24: 62–70.